General Editor: James Gibson

Published:

JANE AUSTEN: **PRIDE AND PREJUDICE** ...
    EMMA Norman Page
    MANSFIELD PARK Richard Wirdnam
ROBERT BOLT: **A MAN FOR ALL SEASONS** Leonard Smith
EMILY BRONTË: **WUTHERING HEIGHTS** Hilda D. Spear
GEOFFREY CHAUCER: **THE PROLOGUE TO THE CANTERBURY TALES**
    Nigel Thomas and Richard Swan
    THE MILLER'S TALE ...
CHARLES DICKENS: **BLEAK HOUSE** Dennis Bu...
    GREAT EXPECTATIONS ...
    HARD TIMES Norman Page
GEORGE ELIOT: **MIDDLEMARCH** Graham Hand...
    SILAS MARNER Graham Hand...
E. M. FORSTER: **A PASSAGE TO INDIA** Hilda D...
THE METAPHYSICAL POETS Joan van Emden
WILLIAM GOLDING: **LORD OF THE FLIES** Raymond Wilson
OLIVER GOLDSMITH: **SHE STOOPS TO CONQUER** Paul Ranger
THOMAS HARDY: **FAR FROM THE MADDING CROWD** Colin Temblett-Wood
    TESS OF THE D'URBERVILLES James Gibson
CHRISTOPHER MARLOWE: **DOCTOR FAUSTUS** David A. Male
ARTHUR MILLER: **THE CRUCIBLE** Leonard Smith
GEORGE ORWELL: **ANIMAL FARM** Jean Armstrong
WILLIAM SHAKESPEARE: **MACBETH** David Elloway
    A MIDSUMMER NIGHT'S DREAM Kenneth Pickering
    ROMEO AND JULIET Helen Morris
    THE WINTER'S TALE Diana Devlin
    HENRY IV PART I Helen Morris
GEORGE BERNARD SHAW: **ST JOAN** Leonée Ormond
RICHARD SHERIDAN: **THE RIVALS** Jeremy Rowe
    THE SCHOOL FOR SCANDAL Paul Ranger

Forthcoming:

SAMUEL BECKETT: **WAITING FOR GODOT** J. Birkett
WILLIAM BLAKE: **SONGS OF INNOCENCE AND SONGS OF EXPERIENCE**
    A. Tomlinson
GEORGE ELIOT: **THE MILL ON THE FLOSS** H. Wheeler
T. S. ELIOT: **MURDER IN THE CATHEDRAL** P. Lapworth
HENRY FIELDING: **JOSEPH ANDREWS** T. Johnson
E. M. FORSTER: **HOWARD'S END** I. Milligan
WILLIAM GOLDING: **THE SPIRE** R. Sumner
THOMAS HARDY: **THE MAYOR OF CASTERBRIDGE** R. Evans
SELECTED POEMS OF GERALD MANLEY HOPKINS
PHILIP LARKIN: **THE WHITSUN WEDDING AND THE LESS DECEIVED**
    A. Swarbrick
D. H. LAWRENCE: **SONS AND LOVERS** R. Draper
HARPER LEE: **TO KILL A MOCKINGBIRD** Jean Armstrong
THOMAS MIDDLETON: **THE CHANGELING** A. Bromham
ARTHUR MILLER: **DEATH OF A SALESMAN** P. Spalding
WILLIAM SHAKESPEARE: **HAMLET** J. Brooks
    HENRY V P. Davison
    KING LEAR F. Casey
    JULIUS CAESAR David Elloway
    MEASURE FOR MEASURE M. Lilly
    OTHELLO Christopher Beddows
    RICHARD II C. Barber
    TWELFTH NIGHT Edward Leeson
    THE TEMPEST Kenneth Pickering
TWO PLAYS OF JOHN WEBSTER David A. Male

Also published by Macmillan

MASTERING ENGLISH LITERATURE R. Gill
MASTERING ENGLISH LANGUAGE S. H. Burton
MASTERING ENGLISH GRAMMAR S. H. Burton

WORK OUT SERIES
WORK OUT ENGLISH LANGUAGE ('O' level and GCSE) S. H. Burton
WORK OUT ENGLISH LITERATURE ('A' level) S. H. Burton

MACMILLAN MASTER GUIDES
THE METAPHYSICAL POETS

JOAN VAN EMDEN

MACMILLAN

First edition 1986

Published by
MACMILLAN EDUCATION LTD
Houndmills, Basingstoke, Hampshire RG21 2XS
and London
Companies and representatives
throughout the world

Typeset by
TecSet, Sutton, Surrey

Printed in Hong Kong

British Library Cataloguing in Publication Data
Van Emden, Joan
The metaphysical poets.—(Macmillan master series)
1. English poetry—Early modern, 1500–1700
History and criticism
I. Title
821'.3'09   PR545.M4
ISBN 0-333-38404-0 Pbk
ISBN 0-333-40224-3 Pbk export

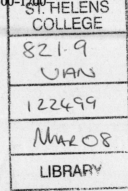

CONTENTS

ACKNOWLEDGEMENTS

The Metaphysical Poets has as its textual basis Jack Dalglish's most useful *Eight Metaphysical Poets*, which skilfully preserves the feeling of the original seventeenth-century writing. In preparing my commentary on the poets and their work, I am especially grateful for the kindness and support of the General Editor of the series, Dr James Gibson.

I should also like to thank, among many friends and colleagues, Lois Mitchison and Reverend Ian Paton for their historical and theological scholarship respectively; I am, as I have long been, indebted to Norah Byron for her encouragement and clear-sighted criticism. My family believed in the book even when I didn't; Ann Redfern and Valerie Andrews typed it expertly and with good humour. I am grateful to them all.

The Metaphysical Poets is dedicated *ad maiorem Dei gloriam*, which would, I hope, please the poets.

JOAN VAN EMDEN

Cover illustration: *George Herbert at Bemerton* by William Dyce. © Guildhall Art Gallery, London, courtesy of the Bridgeman Art Library.

GENERAL EDITOR'S PREFACE

The aim of the Macmillan Master Guides is to help you to appreciate the book you are studying by providing information about it and by suggesting ways of reading and thinking about it which will lead to a fuller understanding. The section on the writer's life and background has been designed to illustrate those aspects of the writer's life which have influenced the work, and to place it in its personal and literary context. The summaries and critical commentary are of special importance in that each brief summary of the action is followed by an examination of the significant critical points. The space which might have been given to repetitive explanatory notes has been devoted to a detailed analysis of the kind of passage which might confront you in an examination. Literary criticism is concerned with both the broader aspects of the work being studied and with its detail. The ideas which meet us in reading a great work of literature, and their relevance to us today, are an essential part of our study, and our Guides look at the thought of their subject in some detail. But just as essential is the craft with which the writer has constructed his work of art, and this is considered under several technical headings — characterisation, language, style and stagecraft.

The authors of these Guides are all teachers and writers of wide experience, and they have chosen to write about books they admire and know well in the belief that they can communicate their admiration to you. But you yourself must read and know intimately the book you are studying. No one can do that for you. You should see this book as a lamp-post. Use it to shed light, not to lean against. If you know your text and know what it is saying about life, and how it says it, then you will enjoy it, and there is no better way of passing an examination in literature.

JAMES GIBSON

1 METAPHYSICAL POETRY

1.1 INTRODUCTION

To meet for the first time great literature from a different age is always exciting and challenging. Our imagination and our sensitivity to the world around us enlarge with our reading: we become richer and more complex in our own natures by contact with those whose gifts have allowed them rare insight, and the ability powerfully to communicate their ideas and emotions to others.

Most of us meet nineteenth-century Romantic poetry at school, and associate poetry with nature and with a poet's own emotional development. Those who have also read eighteenth-century poetry will know that intellect and a cynical view of society can also produce fine poetry, and that hate can generate an emotional outburst which, as in Alexander Pope's writing, conveys its scorching violence to the reader.

Nevertheless to meet the poetry of the seventeenth century, and in particular of the group known as the Metaphysical Poets, is to be challenged in a different way: emotion and intellect are called to action at the same time, and inextricably. As the poets produce a vision of what we may call the 'whole' human being, so they demand a total response.

At first sight, the poetry may seem daunting because some of its references are difficult for a modern reader. We are not familiar with the 'science' of alchemy (the transmutation of base metals into gold), and perhaps find it difficult to appreciate the depth of fear, suspicion and hatred found between Christians whose theological disputes resulted in persecution, imprisonment and even death. If these are ideas alien to our own society, we readily understand, perhaps more easily than the generations between the poets and ourselves, that human beings are not *just* emotional or *just* intellectual, but are composed of body, mind and soul (however we may interpret 'soul') which, as modern medicine and psychology show us, are interrelated and interdependent.

This sense of the wholeness of human life is strong in Metaphysical poetry, and, once difficulties of detail have been overcome, it is enormously attractive to the twentieth century. Human beings are not compartmentalised: they are seen as affected by their emotions, their knowledge and their beliefs. It is this sense of wholeness which is the basis of Metaphysical wit, in that it allows, indeed demands, that disparate parts of experience are brought together to illuminate each other and so to illuminate also our understanding.

The term 'Metaphysical' was allocated to this particular group of poets more or less by accident. John Dryden, writing in an uncomplimentary way of John Donne, said:

> He affects the metaphysics, not only in his satires, but in his amorous verses, where nature only should reign . . .

and Dr Samuel Johnson picked up the word to attach it to 'a race of writers, that may be termed the metaphysical poets'. In spite of later attempts to free the writers concerned from this label, it has stuck, and it has its uses. The dictionary definition of 'metaphysics' is 'theoretical philosophy of being and knowing', and of 'metaphysical' is 'based on abstract general reasoning; over-subtle; incorporeal' (*The Concise Oxford Dictionary*). Obviously, Donne and his fellow poets could not be labelled 'metaphysical' in the usual sense, least of all incorporeal. They are not poets who write of philosophical speculations, as Lucretius, the Roman philosopher and poet, or John Milton did. Yet they are intensely interested in the speculations current in their time, and, as the critic J. B. Leishman among others has pointed out, they use philosophy, theology and popular science in their imagery.

'Use' is the key word. These poets lived at a time of intellectual excitement, and they shared the interests of the educated men and women of their day: medicine, psychology, scientific discovery and geographical exploration were subjects of discussion and debate, and the lively, energetic mind of a man like Donne found the subjects fascinating in themselves and a rich source of illustration in his poetry. We can compare the fascination which madness (and the question of who is truly sane) held for William Shakespeare when he wrote *King Lear*; the idea that courtship might involve the telling of strange stories of faraway people and their customs which we see in *Othello*; the implications of magic in *The Tempest*. It is obvious that Shakespeare too shared the preoccupations of his contemporaries. If 'metaphysical' may be interpreted freely as showing a deep interest in the way in which human beings live, relate to one another and to God, then our poets may indeed be called by that label, however oddly it was first applied.

1.2 POETIC STYLE

From this same universality of interest develops the quality usually called 'Metaphysical wit'. T. S. Eliot defines this efficiently:

> . . . it implies a constant inspection and criticism of experience. It

involves, probably, a recognition, implicit in the expression of every experience, of other kinds of experience which are possible.

Experience is observed from as many different aspects as possible. It will be viewed by the intellect, analysed, dissected, thought through; it will be felt by the emotions, intensely, personally and also at arm's length (as in Andrew Marvell's 'Definition of Love'); it will be linked with the wider question of man's existence, not only with his relationships to other people and other knowledge, but his place in the universe, his place in the time/eternity paradox, his relationship with God.

Donne's treatment of his constant theme, love, may be seen in this way. The most famous example of Metaphysical wit is probably his comparing lovers to a pair of compasses. It is an outrageous, fantastic piece of imagination, and yet it is carefully and logically thought out; the image develops in an intellectually precise way, as if it grows in the mind as the poet is writing and has to be analysed even in the act of creation. At the same time, it is emotionally satisfying: 'such wilt thou be to me' is immediately moving in its simplicity. Not only does the image fulfil all these requirements, but its very outrageousness is entertaining and gives intellectual pleasure. It is 'witty' in the modern sense.

Two equally striking examples of Donne's wit may be enlightening. In 'Twicknam Garden', he describes his '. . . spider love, which transubstantiates all'. The emotion of the poem is violent, aggressive and immediate: the poet is embittered to distraction by the faithfulness of his beloved – to somebody else. Yet the frustrated sexuality of the poem is expressed in a one-word image from folklore (spider) and then by an intellectually perceived analogy, in religious terms. (See the Commentary on this poem.) In Donne's 'Holy Sonnet xiv', the emotion, equally violent and deeply felt, is a religious one: the poet is asking God to force his devotion (with the paradoxical 'yet dearly I love you' showing that the devotion which needs to be forced is already freely given), but the idea of forced love suggests an intellectual analogy with rape which is explicit in the last line.

All experiences inform one another, and the bringing together of diverse experiences is the essence of Metaphysical wit. At the same time, it is founded on logic and analogy, the working out of an exact parallelism (as in Marvell's 'Drop of Dew') or a logical progression (as in the 'if . . .but . . .therefore' of the 'Coy Mistress'). Logic informs, for instance, the analysis of the body/spirit relationship in 'The Extasie', and the development of the bitter jest in 'The Funerall'. The logic may indeed be fallacious, as in the paradox at the heart of 'Holy Sonnet xiv', described above, or the conclusion, more light-heartedly, that 'nothing else is' apart from the lovers, in 'The Sunne Rising', but the dialectic method (a training in argument by debating opposed points of view and resolving them), in which Donne and his contemporaries were educated flowed into the imagination of their writing.

The *conceit* is a particular form of wit: an image which is explored and developed at length, demanding great control and precision on the part of the writer. Marvell's 'Drop of Dew' is a good example of a poem which consists entirely of one such logically patterned, extended image. The poet describes the dewdrop, restless on the rose petal in the early morning, awaiting its evaporation by the sun; the soul is likened to a drop of water from 'the clear Fountain of Eternal Day', a dew-like drop which becomes analogous to the soul, being precariously balanced on the 'humane flow'r' awaiting with eagerness its ascent back to God. In the final four lines of the poem, Marvell takes these two pictures and adds a third, that of 'Manna's Sacred Dew', which is also God-given and, like dewdrop and human soul, is dissolved back into the 'Almighty Sun' which is God. The logic and precision of Marvell's thought produces a poem which both arouses and satisfies the intellect, while fulfilling the religious exploration which it undertakes.

Donne's compasses, discussed above and in the Commentary on his 'Valediction', provide another example of a Metaphysical conceit as, in a briefer form, does his 'voyage of discovery' in the 'Hymne to God my God'.

In contrast to many of his predecessors, Donne uses a direct and often colloquial *diction*, and simplicity of language is especially marked in the later poets George Herbert and Henry Vaughan. Diction combines with a strongly controlled *rhythm* which is closely tied to the meaning: if the result sounds harsh or gentle, it is because the poet deliberately chooses to make his words move in time to their meaning. The apparent childish simplicity of Vaughan's:

> He sayes it is so far
> That he hath quite forgot how to get there,

is the perfect expression of the confusion of man, with his childlike restlessness, described so concisely and effectively later in the same poem: 'Man is the shuttle'.

The simple but heavily stressed words of Donne's 'Nocturnall' express unforgettably the weight of grief: 'For I am every dead thing', while Herbert, master of plain, businesslike language, uses a commercial transaction as the basis of his sonnet, 'Redemption': 'Having been tenant long to a rich Lord. . .' Even when the imagery is based on ideas alien to a modern reader (for instance, the old Ptolemaic system of the universe, with the earth at the centre and the 'sphere' of the sun encircling it), the language is simple enough: 'This bed thy centre is, these walls, thy sphere.' All four poets, incidentally, almost certainly accepted the system of the astronomer, Nicolaus Copernicus (1473–1543), with the earth revolving round the sun, but the old idea was sufficiently well known to be a useful basis for imagery.

As befits the contemporaries of Shakespeare and of the other great dramatists of the late sixteenth and early seventeenth century, the early Metaphysical poets show a striking *dramatic urgency* in their work. In the 1590s, London was the scene of intense literary activity, most of all in the theatre. Robert Greene's lively comedies, John Lyly's decorous plays of exaggerated language and conceit, the majestic poetic drama of Christopher Marlowe combined with the work of prose satirists such as Thomas Nashe to produce an English language which was versatile and robust, stately and formal, flexible and humorous, a wonderful instrument for drama and poetry. Shakespeare, of course, wrote sonnets, long poems and many of his greatest plays (the early comedies, *Romeo and Juliet*, the major histories and the 'dark comedies' such as *Measure for Measure*) during this decade, and it would be surprising if John Donne, the 'frequenter of plays', had not caught something of the vitality of the drama. The sense of immediacy of 'Twicknam Garden' (see the Commentary on that poem), the conversational, dramatic opening of 'The Good-morrow':

> I wonder by my troth, what thou, and I
> Did, till we lov'd?

and the emphatic 'b' sounds which so often begin his poems (such as 'The Sunne Rising' and 'Holy Sonnet xiv') represent a sharp contrast to the regular, smooth-flowing lyrical poetry of the earlier Elizabethan poets such as Henry Howard, Earl of Surrey, or Sir Philip Sydney.

George Herbert, although a quieter, less tormented poet than Donne, can occasionally write with a similar dramatic urgency, as in 'The Collar', and Henry Vaughan, like a playwright, watches his human characters acting out their parts in 'The World'. (See the Commentaries on these poems.)

Many of the poets and playwrights mentioned above, including of course Shakespeare, used the *sonnet* form. Petrarch (1304–74), greatest of Italian sonnet writers, inspired an outpouring of courtly sonnets in England. Unfortunately, the love of Petrarch for his Laura produced conventional subject-matter in his disciples: the remote, unattainable lady, the passionate lover, the impossibility of union, all tended to inspire generalised comment and wearisome cliché; lyrical and pleasant though some of the sonnets were, they too readily led to a stalemate in literary development. The contrast with Donne's 'Holy Sonnets' is marked. These have the same immediacy and sense of personal involvement as have his secular poems, and the techniques so recognisable as his (wide-ranging imagery, dramatic openings, a liking for lists which produce a cumulative effect) are equally clear in his sonnets. (For a more detailed examination of the sonnet form, see the Commentary on the three 'Holy Sonnets' included in Chapter 4.)

In each of the Metaphysical poets, there is a sensitivity to the *patterns of ordinary speech*. The simple word order used by Vaughan in 'Man', and Donne's bell-tolling stresses in the 'Nocturnall' have already been mentioned; Herbert's extended conversation-poem 'Love' and Marvell's variation of pace in 'To his Coy Mistress' all show the poets' command of the tempi of speech, the flexibility and agility of the human voice; the stress is always where the voice and the logic of the poem would naturally put it.

If it were possible to sum up the essential quality of Metaphysical poetry in one word, that word would be 'energy'. There is an energy of mind and emotion in all four poets which demands a similarly energetic response in the reader. It is seen in the drama of Donne and Herbert in particular, the poetry bursting forth with a vitality which provokes the reader's emotion:

> Busie old foole, unruly Sunne,
> Why dost thou thus,
> Through windowes, and through curtaines call on us?

or:

> I struck the board, and cry'd, No more.
> I will abroad.

The same energy is seen in the analysis of the quality of love: 'Inter-assured of the mind', or

> Magnanimous Despair alone
> Could show me so divine a thing,

and it is seen in intellectual debate, whether in a secular poem such as 'The Extasie' or in religious terms in 'Satyre iii'.

An energy of mind is able also to produce an apparently simple poem with depth of implication, as in Marvell's 'Little T.C.', where the awareness of time and death underlie the gentle courtly love poem. It will enjoy a pun, even in the most solemn circumstances, as in the play on Donne's own name in 'A Hymne to God the Father', or pour forth sheer enjoyment of life and love:

> My vegetable love should grow
> Vaster than Empires, and more slow,

although, in true Metaphysical style, the enjoyment of hyperbole is transformed instantaneously into horrifying reality:

> . . .then Worms shall try
> That long preserv'd Virginity.

The intellectual energy which enables Marvell to consider, balance and judge both King Charles I and Oliver Cromwell, in the 'Horatian Ode', may seem very far from the ecstatic joy of Vaughan in 'The Morning-Watch', with its perfection in one all-embracing, seemingly simple image:

> . . .Prayer is
> The world in tune.

but both come from the same source, the excitement of mental and emotional analogy, perceived and precisely expressed.

1.3 CONCLUSION

The Metaphysical poets bind the ultimate and the everyday, fusing intellect and imagination and refining both through experience. The multi-faceted life which they express demands an energetic response of mind, body and soul. The modern reader may not be prepared for such a challenge, but if we accept it we will surely find our energy stimulated and our vision of the wholeness of life enriched.

2 LIVES AND LITERARY CONTEXTS

The study of a particular poet, or even of a group of poets, in isolation from their predecessors and contemporaries is always dangerous. It results in the impression that the individual poet invented his or her style without reference to the past, and used ideas without discussing them with friends and fellow writers. Donne especially inherited a tradition and transformed it, but he did so in the spirit of his age, which was very different from that of Marvell who died nearly half a century after the older poet. It is interesting to note how long the Metaphysical tradition lasted: over a century separates the birth of John Donne (1572) from the death of Andrew Marvell (1678).

This chapter will, therefore, look at some of the main trends in seventeenth-century literature to show the similarities and differences which bind the four poets to, or separate them from, other writers of the time. Within this context, the lives of the poets will be outlined: more detailed biographies are readily available elsewhere.

2.1 EDUCATION AND SCHOLARSHIP

There are areas of knowledge which were common to all four poets. Biblical learning was the earliest and most deeply ingrained, whatever their parentage: Donne's learning was Catholic, Herbert's and Vaughan's was Anglican and Marvell's father was a Puritan minister. Religion was central to their lives and to their education. We may take for granted thorough knowledge of the Bible, of theology and of the Prayer Book, as well as familiarity with the books of sermons and treatises popular throughout the century.

All four were also well-educated young men, of some academic distinction (although Vaughan left the scholarship of London for Wales on the outbreak of the Civil War). Their knowledge of the classics (Latin rather than Greek) was profound, and they wrote poetry in Latin as well as translating Latin poetry into English. The sources, for example, of Marvell's 'To his Coy Mistress' show the width of his scholarship (see the Commentary on that poem).

University education – and all four poets went to Oxford or Cambridge – trained young men in rhetoric, skill in debate, and in the logical exposition of classical texts (in which Herbert's abilities were so pronounced that he was appointed Public Orator of the University, which position usually led to high office in the State). The complexity of thought and word-play which is so marked in these poets must have been developed partly by their education. History, philosophy and mathematics were also part of the university system, and Donne and Vaughan both at some time studied law.

'Travel,' wrote the essayist Francis Bacon, 'is a part of education' and except for Vaughan our poets travelled on the Continent and learnt the appropriate languages, Italian being of particular importance because of the influence of Petrarch and contemporary Italian poets. Both Donne and Marvell took part in diplomatic missions abroad and were noted for their eloquence. The combination of religious, classical and European scholarship with rhetoric and philosophy produced the range of learning which we think of as belonging to the Renaissance, and this learning was the inheritance of all four poets.

2.2 DRAMA, POETRY AND PROSE IN THE SEVENTEENTH CENTURY

The excitement of the London theatre in the 1590s has already been described in Chapter 1, and Donne, who became a law student in 1592, took full advantage of new plays, playwrights and theatre buildings. We do not know whether he ever met Shakespeare, but he must have become aware of the possibilities for dramatic effect combined with exquisite poetry which were presented not only in Shakespeare's plays but also, for instance, in those of Christopher Marlowe, whose poetry perhaps reached its height in *Doctor Faustus* (c. 1592) and whose dramatic skills were clearly seen in his last play, *Edward II*, written shortly before his death in 1593.

Shakespeare's major tragedies date from the early years of the reign of King James I, who came to the throne in 1603; the group of so-called 'last plays', including *The Tempest*, were written between approximately 1610 and 1615. At this high point in the drama, the links between theatre and poetry can be seen not only in the use of words and 'conversational' effects, but also in a growing interest in what would nowadays be called 'psychology': the melancholy, self-torturing Hamlet is kin to the tormented, guilt-ridden Donne of the 'Holy Sonnets'. The Jacobean age increasingly produced plays of bitter cynicism and flamboyant violence, combined at their best (for instance, in the work of John Webster, (1580-1634) with poetry of a high quality. Although John Ford (1586-1640) continued to write similar plays into the reign of King Charles I, social and moral satire became more influential: Ben Jonson, Donne's friend and fellow-poet, wrote satires which are still performed and enjoyed, such as

Volpone (1606) and *The Alchemist* (1610). Masques (dramatic presentations of music and verse, often with elaborate scenic effects) were popular at Court, where Charles I and his Queen, Henrietta Maria, sometimes took part in the performances.

The poetic tradition which Donne entered was influenced by the Continent and in particular by Italy (see Chapter 1); the Elizabethan tradition epitomised by Edmund Spenser (1552-99), who wrote the highly decorative epic *The Faerie Queene* in the 1590s, continued alongside the growing influence of the more concentrated and vivid poetry of Jonson and, later, Donne. Jonson was close to Donne in terms of friendship and mutual admiration. There are great differences in their styles: Jonson is more formal, distanced and classical, Donne more colloquial, dramatic and witty, but their combined influence was felt late into the seventeenth century, and in particular on the group known as the Cavalier Poets, so described for their lives at Court rather than their political affiliation. This group produced an elegant and less personal form of poetry, although its best-known representative, Thomas Carew (1594-1640), testifies forcefully to Donne's originality and power in his famous 'Elegie upon the Death of the Deane of Pauls, Dr John Donne'.

The essays of Francis Bacon (1561-1626) have already been quoted; he represented the new 'scientific' spirit of enquiry, and his fine prose, like that of Sir Thomas Browne (1605-82) became increasingly influential. The seventeenth century is, however, sharply divided by the Civil War; at its outbreak in 1642 the theatres were closed and remained so until the Restoration of Charles II in 1660. Poetry became less prominent than political and philosophical writing such as that of the Royalist, materialist and mathematician Thomas Hobbes (1588-1679), who saw man as without innate moral sense; in his most famous work, *Leviathan* (1651), he looked at the realities of political power in terms of conformity demanded by the State. The most widely-read form of literature was perhaps the political or social pamphlet. John Milton (1608-74) wrote such pamphlets with a grandeur and complexity of style which prefigured the epic poem (*Paradise Lost* was probably completed about 1665). The subject matter of his pamphlets was, however, of immediate contemporary interest: the freedom of the press, the tenure of kings and magistrates, the justification for the execution of King Charles I.

The relationship between John Milton and the last of the Metaphysical poets, Andrew Marvell, was a close one, and will be discussed in the survey of Marvell's life. From both a historical and a literary point of view, the years spanned by the four major Metaphysical poets were of unparalleled excitement and action, from the heights of the Shakespearean theatre under James I to the epic poetry of Milton during the Civil War and after the Restoration of the monarchy.

There was much to be read and listened to during the years of the poets' most productive writing, and only a few of the influences to which they were open have been mentioned here. They would not have quarrelled with the comment of that philosopher-statesman, Sir Francis Bacon,

George Herbert's friend, in his *Essays* published in 1597 and, with additions, in 1612:

> Read not to contradict and confute, not to believe and take for granted, not to find talk and discourse, but to weigh and consider. . . reading maketh a full man; conference a ready man; and writing an exact man.

2.3 JOHN DONNE (1572-1631)

John Donne was born in London in 1572, into a strongly Roman Catholic family. His father was a prosperous ironmonger; his mother was the daughter of a popular dramatist, John Heywood, and descended from the sister of Sir Thomas More, executed by King Henry VIII for his refusal to accept the supremacy of the Crown over the Church (see Chapter 3). Donne's father died when he was a small boy, but his mother survived her son, spending some of the later years of her life at the Deanery of St Paul's, a strange residence for so constant a Catholic.

We are told by Izaak Walton, later friend, parishioner and first biographer of Donne, that the boy was educated by a private tutor and then at Oxford, although his Catholicism prevented his taking a degree, as it debarred him from public office. The family's devotion cost them more: the poet's uncle, a Jesuit priest, was imprisoned and sentenced to permanent exile; his younger brother Henry was imprisoned in Newgate for harbouring a Catholic priest, and died there of gaol fever.

So John Donne was confronted with the most critical question of his life: he could remain a Catholic, with the frustrations inevitable for a gifted young man, and with the possibility of a fate similar to his brother's, or he could join the Established Church, and so have open to him all the opportunities which his abilities and ambitions offered. Walton records something of the cost of his decision to become a member of the Church of England: long hours of study and thought, a deep need to find 'truth' (as he describes in 'Satyre iii') and much self-questioning. It was a terrible decision, but once it had been taken, Donne could be employed as Secretary to Sir Thomas Egerton, the Lord High Chancellor, with whose son he had become friendly while they were both with Essex's expeditions to Cadiz and the Azores in 1596-7.

Donne's future at last seemed secure, but he ruined all hope of preferment by secretly marrying Lady Egerton's niece, Ann More; as far as we can tell, the marriage was a happy one, but Walton records its immediate effects in Donne's own words: 'John Donne, Ann Donne, un-done.' He was dismissed by Sir Thomas and imprisoned by Ann's father; much of his small fortune was spent effecting a reunion with his wife and a partial reconciliation to her family, but his employment had gone, and for some years he had to support himself, his wife and their growing family by small allowances and gifts, and by writing verses in celebration of people of wealth and influence.

These were years of poverty and struggle, and very different from the study, play-going and visiting of ladies which had been his occupations when he studied law; he now cultivated the great in the hope of a position which did not materialise. His writings about religious controversy, however, especially the anti-Catholic 'Pseudo-Martyr' of 1610, came to the attention of the King, James I, himself no mean theologian. James desired the poet to become a priest, but to his credit he first refused, feeling unworthy because of his past life, and no doubt also troubled, as he was all his life, by the guilt and melancholy resulting from his change of faith. After another great mental and spiritual battle, Donne eventually accepted ordination in 1615.

Whatever his past or his agonies of conscience, there is no doubt of the depth of Donne's faith or the dedication he brought to his new vocation. In spite of ill-health and deep distress at his wife's death in 1617, he became one of England's greatest preachers, and his sermons, especially those delivered at St Paul's after he became Dean in 1621, are part of the great literature of the age. Some, although probably not all, of his religious poetry was written after his ordination, and it shows clearly that the depressive spirit which was part of his nature, and the guilt of his change of faith, remained to bring him at times close to despair.

In 1631, knowing he was dying, he prepared himself physically and mentally: he had written and preached much about death, and faced it with equanimity and faith.

2.4 GEORGE HERBERT (1593-1633)

To a large extent, George Herbert shared the literary background of John Donne. Socially, they came from very different families, and Herbert had no problems about 'truth'; intellectually, their upbringing was not dissimilar, although Herbert lacked Donne's fascination with the discoveries, geographical and astronomical, of the time. Perhaps the years which separated their births, as well as temperamental differences, made this inevitable. Herbert's range is smaller and his tone gentler, but fine scholarship can be seen in his poetry, even if it is less flamboyant than Donne's.

George Herbert was born in 1593, into a cultured and well-connected family, related to the Earls of Pembroke; George's elder brother Edward, later Lord Herbert of Cherbury, was diplomat, scholar and poet. Probably the strongest influence on the life of George himself was that of his mother, a remarkable woman of beauty, scholarship and piety. After his father's death, she took her children to London and brought them up with care and diligence.

Magdalen Herbert's influence was not confined to her own family. Her home became a centre of culture, and she befriended Donne and his wife after the disasters consequent upon their marriage. Izaak Walton, Herbert's biographer as well as Donne's, refers to the two poets as having 'a long and dear friendship, made up by a sympathy of inclination. . .'. It was through Herbert's mother that they became such friends, and Donne's influence on Herbert's writing is clear.

While at Cambridge, Herbert dedicated his poetic gifts to 'God's glory' and indeed all his poetry is closely tied to his faith and its working out in his daily life. His scholarship was outstanding, and after lecturing in Rhetoric, he became Public Orator at Cambridge, and seemed destined for high office.

Quite why this destiny was not fulfilled is not clear. Herbert had good looks, charm, intellect and good family; he was and remained a member of the Established Church. His mother remarried, and the wealth, culture and influence of Sir John Danvers, his stepfather, must also have helped the young man, whose relations with Sir John were always very good. He was ambitious, and the picture of himself and his own ambitions in 'The Pearl' is not exaggerated. Yet preferment at Court eluded him, in spite of the trouble he took to gain the favours of James I.

In 1625, at the time of King James' death, which may have had something to do with his decision, Herbert left the Court and chose to become a priest. Perhaps the vocation had always been in his mind, as his early poems suggest, and perhaps the influence of Donne, then Dean of St Paul's and a frequent visitor to the Danvers household, was a deciding factor. There was also a period of ill-health immediately after his ordination which might suggest yet another partial reason for his leaving the Court; it was some time before he took up parish life.

Herbert visited Lord Danby, his stepfather's brother, in 1628, and there he met Jane Danvers, cousin of his host. They were married within a few days of meeting, a step which, as Walton records, would have seemed rash if they had not been so well suited. Certainly, when Herbert became Rector of Bemerton near Salisbury, in 1630, Jane was a model of quiet service and devotion to her husband and the parish, and Walton was sufficiently impressed to give a short biography of her widowhood and subsequent remarriage, at the end of his 'Life' of her husband.

The last three years of Herbert's life were devoted to his parishioners, by whom he was regarded almost as a saint, and to his fellow priests, for whom he wrote his prose work *A Priest to the Temple* and some of his poetry. He became known and loved throughout the area, and Walton tells of his humble and generous actions and the high esteem in which he was held. Endearingly, he also records the poet's twice-weekly visits to Salisbury to make music, in which 'he was a most excellent master'. The poetry and prose which he wrote at Bemerton testify to both his love of music and his dedication to his calling.

George Herbert was not yet forty when he died of consumption in 1633, deeply mourned by family, friends and parishioners. Whatever the strange path which led the gifted, scholarly young courtier to become the saintly priest of a small country parish, the transformation seems to have been a satisfying one, and to have produced poetry for which his readers will continue to be grateful.

2.5 HENRY VAUGHAN (1621-95)

Henry Vaughan was Welsh by birth and in a sense also by choice, associating himself with the 'Silures', the local Welsh tribe so-called under the Romans. He was born in 1621, one of twin sons of a small landowner of aristocratic descent, distantly related to the family of George Herbert. After studying at Oxford, he moved to London as a student of law, but at the beginning of the Civil War in 1642, he returned to Wales to spend the rest of his life there. We do not know how active a part he played in the war, but as a Royalist and a member of the Church of England, he and his family were probably persecuted in minor ways under locally fierce Puritan authority.

These years were difficult, too, as a result of illness, financial worries, and the death of a younger brother, and it may have been this combination of circumstances which made the poet open to the two dominant influences on his later writing, the 'holy life and verse' of George Herbert, which brought about what Vaughan called a religious conversion, and a growing understanding of and love for the wild beauty of the Welsh countryside.

In 1646, Vaughan married, and settled on his father's estate at Newton; in 1653, his wife died and he subsequently married her sister. The children of these two marriages quarrelled about their inheritance, and Vaughan became burdened with lawsuits among his family. Fortunately, his practice as a doctor (we do not know where he qualified) flourished, and he spent the last years living a quiet but busy life in his beloved countryside, where he died in 1695.

2.6 ANDREW MARVELL (1621-78)

Andrew Marvell was born in 1621, in Winestead, near Hull, in the East Riding of Yorkshire. He was the son of the vicar and started life in a small rural community, but he was only three when the family moved to Hull on his father's appointment as Lecturer of Holy Trinity Church and Master of Hull Grammar School, which the young Andrew attended. From his father, he gained a Puritan outlook, eloquence and a devotion to duty which brought both father and son esteem and admiration.

At Cambridge, the young poet found himself part of an intellectual circle in which ideas about literature and religion were constantly discussed. A powerful group of Jesuits temporarily converted Marvell to Catholicism and he ran off to London, where he was caught by his father and restored to the Anglican Church and Cambridge. In 1642, after his father's death, Marvell travelled widely on the Continent, becoming proficient in a range of languages and avoiding, by accident or design, the Civil War, although his sympathies seem to have been Royalist.

If we take 1630 as effectively the end of the literary work of Donne and Herbert, and allow that Vaughan stands apart from the other Metaphysical poets in his Welsh isolation, we find a twenty-year gap before the most productive period of Andrew Marvell's writing. These years, 1630–50, are crucially important in British history, including most of the reign of Charles I, the Civil War, King Charles' execution and the beginnings of the Commonwealth under Oliver Cromwell. Religiously, the Church of England was transformed from the Established Church to a body oppressed and persecuted by the Puritans (see Chapter 3 for a more detailed consideration of the historical and religious background). Andrew Marvell was influenced by the pre-Civil War poets, most of all by Donne and Jonson, but the themes of his poetry were often contemporary.

By 1650, Marvell was a moderate Parliamentarian (but with the balanced judgement of that courageous and essentially sane poem 'The Horatian Ode') and became tutor to Mary Fairfax, daughter of Lord Fairfax who had been Cromwell's military Commander but who, in opposition to the execution of Charles I, and to further bloodshed in Scotland, had resigned and retired to his estates at Nun Appleton in Yorkshire. The gardens there, the congenial company and the cultured lifestyle combined to make the right setting for the production of some of Marvell's best poetry, not least that which showed his abhorrence of civil war (as in 'Upon Appleton House'). We cannot be sure how or when Marvell came to know John Milton (although both had Yorkshire connections), but in 1653 Milton tried to get a government post for the younger poet; he was unsuccessful, and Marvell became tutor to Cromwell's ward William Dutton, living at the Oxenbridge household at Eton (see 'Bermudas'). In 1657, he became Latin Secretary, assisting the blind Milton, and in 1659, after Cromwell's death, he was elected MP for Hull, remaining so until he died.

The relationship between the great epic poet Milton and Marvell, his assistant, is an interesting one. Marvell venerated the older man, but did not follow either his extreme Puritanism or his support for the execution of Charles I. Milton's pre-Civil War poetry has some of the elements which we recognise in Marvell, such as the use of colour and the emotionally-distanced discussion of love, but from about 1638 onwards, Milton moves towards the weighty, classical grandeur of *Paradise Lost*, far removed from the urbane sophistication of Marvell's finest writing. Nor does Marvell easily fit the Puritan label, although he would no doubt have accepted it. His faith was deep, and the lovely description of the Christian soul in 'On a Drop of Dew' reveals his sensitive and thoughtful understanding of the soul's aspiration to unity with God. It is not, any more than is 'Bermudas', a Puritan poem. Marvell's love of beauty, of the rich colour of gardens, of friendship and of good wine separate him from the narrow Calvinism which Milton, at least most of the time, adhered to.

After the Restoration in 1660, Marvell was sent abroad on diplomatic missions, and seems to have accepted the restored monarchy while reserving his right to criticise it, sometimes at considerable personal risk. His generosity and loyalty are evident in his public and lively support of the disgraced Milton, and it is in no small measure due to Marvell's influence that Milton lived in freedom to write *Paradise Lost*. He is described by contemporaries as being a noted wit, fashionably dressed, modest in conversation, choosing his friends with care. Unusually for his time, he was an excellent constituency MP, keeping the citizens of Hull well-informed about events in Parliament, and travelling back regularly to his home town. His famous words about the Civil War, 'I think the Cause was too good to have been fought for', show the man of peace; the occasion on which he came to blows in the House of Commons with a fellow member, and was removed by the Speaker, shows him also to have had something of a hot temper and a ready tongue (he got his own back verbally on the Speaker the next day). Most of his political pamphleteering was anonymous (wisely, in an age of strict and sometimes brutal censorship), but when his life was threatened, he signed his name to his most famous satire, 'The Rehearsal Transprosed'.

Marvell died in 1678; his poetry was published in 1681; his epitaph in St Giles in the Fields, London, speaks of his wit and learning, and strength of judgement. It is a fair comment.

2.7 CONCLUSION

When Andrew Marvell followed Cromwell's coffin in 1658, his fellow-mourner had been John Dryden (1631-1700), master of satire and the mock-heroic. With Dryden, and with the Restoration theatre of Wycherley, Otway and Congreve, literature became public and social, its themes became personalities and the conventions of society. The Metaphysical blend of wit and personal devotion was left far behind.

3 THEMES AND ISSUES

3.1 CONTEMPORARY THEMES

Donne inherited more than richness of language: he took and transformed themes which had been used not only by the Elizabethans but often by ancient Greek writers. Some of his originality of treatment and immediacy of impact comes from personal experience, for instance of early death (Donne's wife and several of his children died young; see also Marvell's 'Picture of Little T. C.'), and of the conflict between the writer or artist creating within time the work which will outlast him.

Time is a constant burden. Shakespeare refers to 'Devouring Time' in one of his sonnets, and to 'Envious and calumniating time' in Troilus and Cressida. The Metaphysical poets shared the sense of the transience of earthly life (as in Donne's 'Song') and belief in eternal life (as in Donne's 'Holy Sonnet x'). Vaughan especially shows in 'The World' the conflict of the individual faced with the attractions of earthly existence and the 'Ring of pure and endless light' to which man might aspire.

The Metaphysical poets believed, as did the Greeks before them, that time, the enemy of man, could be defeated, and the most energetic and forceful expression of that defeat is probably in the last lines of Marvell's 'Coy Mistress', when the lovers gain the victory by making time 'run' at their bidding. Love, the theme of so much contemporary poetry, is indeed the enemy of death, whether in God-given eternal life or by the constancy of the human lover (as in Donne's 'Nocturnall'). Love may be joyful, cynical, embittered, grieving; above all, it may be a relationship between human beings and between man and God, but it is seen as a unity of body, mind and spirit. Donne discusses the body/soul interdependence explicitly in 'The Extasie'. Love, whether human or divine, is an essential part of real life, and there is no idealisation or sentimentality in this poetry: the poet of 'The Funerall' is as cynical as his mistress is faithless; Vaughan looks at humankind with clear-sighted affection in 'The World', and Marvell analyses the quality and impossibility of an ideal love in his 'Definition'.

Donne, like his contemporaries, is interested in *order*, the divinely-inspired organisation of the universe, and in his 'Nocturnall' he shows us the hierarchy of creation, from God (via the angels) to man, beasts, plants, inanimate objects, to the incorporeal (in this case, the shadow). Vaughan finds a harmony in the natural world (see the Commentary on 'The Morning-Watch'), and the idea of the universe obeying the ordered direction of God (clearly shown in Vaughan's 'Man') underlies much Metaphysical poetry.

This sense of *harmony* has to be held in tension with the 'modern' knowledge of the earth and other planets revolving round the sun, rather than the earth as the centre of the universe. This new *astronomy*, put forward by Galileo (1564–1642), was accepted by many educated people although the old idea was useful as a source of poetic imagery (as in Donne's 'The Sunne Rising'). A new order in the universe inevitably led to a *'new Philosophy'*, which, as Donne himself declared, called 'all in doubt.' Galileo was at odds with the Church's traditional teaching, and only gradually did his scientific knowledge gain ascendancy over the old order; it was difficult for Donne's contemporaries to accept that man was not both at the centre of the universe and also midway between God and lower forms of creation. Sir Francis Bacon, in his *Advancement of Learning* (1605) advocated a 'scientific' approach to knowledge, based on *reason*; by the mid-seventeenth century Marvell's contemporary, the poet and scientist Abraham Cowley, was one of the founders of the Royal Society. The 'new Philosophy' had become generally accepted.

The natural world was considered and discussed as part of philosophical thinking, but only in Vaughan do we find the observation and appreciation of *nature* itself. The awareness of God as Creator and of man's ability to see the power of God through nature radiates through Vaughan's mystical poetry: his imagery is often of light, water, mist, budding flowers, all carefully and precisely observed in his Welsh countryside. Marvell is the poet of *cultivated nature*, of gardens with ordered ranks of trees and floral clocks; his close observation is of the dew on a rose petal rather than of the mist over the mountains.

Behind all these aspects of contemporary thought is a close knowledge of both biblical teaching and Church doctrine. The relationship of God and man is a fundamental theme for all these poets, and will be discussed in greater detail later in this chapter.

3.2 HISTORICAL AND RELIGIOUS BACKGROUND

In order to understand the lives and attitudes of the Metaphysical poets, it is important to recognise the centrality of religion in the thought and practice of the seventeenth century. To our own age, this may seem strange, but the apathy or mild hostility towards religion often found in twentieth-century British society is far removed from the attitude of the poets and their contemporaries. Faith and hostility abounded, but the hostility was of one kind of faith towards another; apathy, certainly among the educated and probably among the general public, would have been unthinkable.

The Metaphysical poets have widely different attitudes to religion, from the Catholicism of Donne's youth to the Puritanism of Marvell, but they were all deeply involved with the ideas of their time and would have read, listened to and discussed controversial aspects of religious belief with friends and fellow scholars.

Donne, in his 'Satyre iii', sums up what all four poets would probably have subscribed to:

> To stand inquiring right, is not to stray,
> To sleepe or runne wrong, is.

The search for truth and the discovery of a right relationship between man and God are crucial in the thinking of each of them; the sin would have been apathy.

There are perhaps two overwhelming reasons for this prevalence of religion. Firstly, the Church was at the centre of the life of the local community, and had been for a long time. To a largely uneducated population, it represented the learning that mattered (God's will); to a largely rural and poverty-stricken people, it represented a meeting place, colour and drama (often literally: the medieval drama, based largely on biblical stories and 'morality' teaching, came from and centred on the Church, although increasingly lay people were involved in its organisation). Secondly, religion was inextricably bound up with politics. Before the Reformation, the Church owned about a quarter of England, the leaders of the Church were rich in status as well as money and property, and the Church's laws controlled even the finances of the ordinary layman (he paid his tithes, one tenth of all his produce, to his rector, and could be imprisoned if he failed to do so). The Church's own courts had control over many areas of life which affected him, while the clergy were largely exempted from the penalties imposed by the ordinary secular courts. The relationship between King and Pope, often an uneasy one, influenced the politics of the State; the relationship between the local Church or monastery and the laymen who might well be employed by the Church to work on Church land influenced and indeed controlled much of daily life.

Division within the Church was not, therefore, a remote and purely academic matter, but one of immediate concern, even of life and death, to lay Christians as well as to the clergy. The causes of the Reformation, the movement which split the Church into Catholic and Protestant divisions, are too complex to be discussed fully here. Although the sixteenth century was a period of great devotion, there was discontent among some of the laity at abuses of clerical power. The great wealth of bishops and of the monasteries contrasted with the poverty of most of the people. In an age of growing literacy and a desire for education among the more prosperous laymen, there was some discontent at the local level in spite of the close bonds which often linked laity and clergy. The rector or vicar might be away dealing with one of his other parishes or with administrative affairs, while the work of the parish devolved on the curate, who was often ignorant and underpaid; while the powerful clergy were equal to the nobility in wealth, some curates earned no more than unskilled labourers.

In England, the combination of the rapid spread of printed material and the availability of the Bible and other religious books in the language of ordinary people resulted in questioning and unhappiness at the state of the Church, based for the first time on knowledge held by a minority, but an increasingly vocal minority, of the population.

The Reformation developed first, and with much deep-rooted bitterness, on the Continent, through the work of scholars like Desiderius Erasmus, who was Dutch, attacking abuses within the Church and demanding the availability of the Bible to all. He visited England several times and influenced thinkers of the day, including Sir Thomas More. Eventually, More was to become Lord Chancellor and to die rather than acknowledge King Henry VIII as head of the English Church. His sister was the grandmother of John Donne, and so a link between Reformation thinking and Catholic faith was already forged in the poet's family.

However, it was the giant ability and force of character of the German, Martin Luther (to whom Donne refers in 'Satyre iii', 1. 97), which advanced the Reformation to the point of a break with the Roman Catholic Church. Luther was a scholar of great personal faith and integrity, who attacked the Church from the basis of biblical teaching, even preaching that obedience to Pope or bishop was secondary to the individual's understanding of the faith. His writings were translated and read throughout Europe, and his followers became known (against his will) as Lutherans. Other Reformation leaders, notably John Calvin in Geneva (the inspiration of 'Crantz', in 'Satyre iii', 1. 49), carried Luther's ideas further. Calvin himself was a learned and a pious man, but his writings moved increasingly away from Catholicism, and formed the basis of Puritan activism in England as well as in his home country. (See the section 'Belief', later in this chapter.)

The Reformers were international in their discussions and in their writing; the development of national Churches, as in England, is to a certain extent a by-product. The stress on the individual conscience and on scriptural teaching was attractive to many, especially later among the emerging middle class, but the familiarity and the solidity of the Catholic Church remained its strongest protection.

It was Henry VIII who in England broke the ties between the English Church and the Papacy. His first leading minister was Thomas Wolsey, lowly born (which was held against him by his enemies), but eventually uniting the authority of a Cardinal of the Church with the power of a Lord Chancellor. He became exceedingly rich and was exceedingly arrogant, and harrassed even the comparatively poor with taxation. Wolsey did little to endear his Church to the English people, and although he was in a position to make reforms in the Church and talked frequently of doing so, in practice he did little which was not designed to advance his own position.

The downfall of Wolsey and the break with Rome are closely linked.

Henry's first wife, Catherine of Aragon, had borne only a daughter, Mary, and Henry wanted to annul their marriage in order to marry Anne Boleyn. It was assumed that the Pope would bow to political pressure, but Wolsey failed to reach a swift settlement, and pressure mounted for the King to take the law into his own hands. The Commons under Thomas Cromwell and the Church under Thomas Cranmer (both Protestant thinkers) supported Henry, and Cranmer finally annulled the marriage himself and Henry married Anne. The Pope thereupon excommunicated Henry, depriving him of the Sacraments of the Church (and therefore of the hope of redemption).

In 1534 the Act of Supremacy was passed, affirming Henry as 'Supreme Head of the Church of England', and the specifically Protestant element grew in religious and political importance. Treason now included speaking against the King's title (including his title as Head of the Church), outspoken opponents of the divorce were executed, monasteries were dissolved and the nation as a whole, afraid of the sin of treason, acquiesced, if only in the name of civil peace.

Henry VIII was succeeded in 1547 by his son Edward VI, who was only a minor; the country was governed in effect by his uncles, Somerset and Northumberland. Both the king and his uncles were Protestant, and Cranmer's tolerance ensured that there were only two executions for heresy (either denying accepted Church doctrine or proclaiming beliefs repudiated by the Church) during the six years of Edward's reign. The new Prayer Book of 1549 was essentially Protestant but tactfully ambiguous. In 1552, however, Parliament introduced a more extreme Prayer Book, reflecting a strongly Protestant doctrine.

Edward died in 1553, and was succeeded briefly by Lady Jane Grey, who was executed for treason in spite of her innocence, and then by his sister Mary. The latter had general support despite her Catholicism and her official bastardy (the marriage of her mother Catherine to Henry VIII having been annulled). The Reformation was slowing down on the Continent, and on the whole, people were glad to get back to the old, familiar faith. Parliament reversed Henry's and Edward's Protestant legislation. Mary urgently needed to marry and produce an heir to ensure the Catholic succession. Unfortunately for her popularity, she chose to marry Philip, heir to Spain and the Netherlands, and she failed to have a child. By the end of her reign, the economic state of the country was the worst of the century, which further undermined her position.

Laws against heresy, now Protestant heresy, were revived and vigorously enforced, and many Protestants, among them Cranmer, were burnt. Most of those who died in this way were ordinary men and women of humble birth but strong in the Protestant faith, and there was organised public resentment against the combination of the Spanish marriage with such ruthless persecution. Many well-to-do Protestants fled abroad (especially to Switzerland and Germany) and underground churches were founded in the south east, particularly in London.

Nevertheless, on the Continent as in England, a measure of Catholic reform and revival was in progress. It is interesting that all except one of Mary's bishops refused to take the Oath of Supremacy to the Protestant Queen Elizabeth (who had the good sense not to make martyrs of them). Eventually and reluctantly, Mary had to acknowledge that by Henry VIII's will, her younger half-sister Elizabeth was her heir; Mary died in 1558, and Protestantism returned to England.

The effect of so much change and counter-change was to start a polarisation of opinion. Elizabeth herself was not strongly either Catholic or Protestant; she seems to have felt that the exact nature of faith was between the individual and God. She was also 'by authority of Parliament' given the title of 'Supreme Governor' (not Head) of the Church of England, and this strengthened her position by allowing more recognition of her reign by continental Catholic monarchs. Nevertheless, her Council included a strongly Protestant party and a group of returned exiles of Puritan disposition, and popular feeling became increasingly anti-Catholic.

The official Elizabethan Church was now meeting growing opposition from both Catholics and Calvinists, both of whom attacked it as being a man-made institution with no historical basis. It was important that such charges were refuted, and the greatest defender of the Elizabethan Church, Richard Hooker, wrote effectively and skilfully to assert its links with the early Church, presenting it as a return to true religion rather than as innovation.

At the time of Hooker's writing, the young Catholic John Donne was living and studying in London. Against such a background, not least his own family's suffering for its Catholic faith, we can imagine the pressures put on a young man of great ability and intellect, denied a degree at the end of his university studies, denied any kind of preferment at Court, denied office under Elizabeth, apparently condemned to a life of frustration because of his faith. At the same time, as we can clearly see from 'Satyre iii', he was influenced by men like Hooker in wanting to find 'truth': his plea to himself and his contemporaries to 'seeke true religion' must have been shared by many in his position. By the end of Elizabeth's reign he had accepted the Established Church, although the questioning and self-torture were to remain all his life, influencing especially his later religious poetry.

Donne was probably fortunate in the new King, James I. At his accession, Catholics were still numerous, but lacking in any kind of influence. As Catholic priests could not acknowledge the supremacy of Elizabeth, they were guilty of treason, and many priests and those who helped them (including, of course, Donne's younger brother) had died for their faith with great courage and devotion. At the death of Elizabeth, priests in exile hurried back, and their numbers increased dramatically in the first years of James' reign. James himself, who was married to a Catholic, was well disposed to Catholicism, although his tolerance was not helped by the Gunpowder Plot and other manifestations of Catholic intrigue.

Nevertheless, James wanted to achieve peace and some sort of unity in his Church, and his coming to the throne raised hopes for concessions among both Roman Catholics and members of the Church of England. He attempted a dialogue with the Puritans at the Hampton Court Conference of 1604. He authorised a new translation of the Bible (known now as the Authorised Version or the King James Bible) and took an intelligent interest in religious discussion. Sadly, any hope of a unified, broadly-based Jacobean Church was broken under pressure from the House of Commons, which pressed James to increase and enforce the anti-Catholic laws. Roman Catholics were rigorously punished for recusancy, the refusal to attend the services of the Established Church. On the other side, James' Archbishop of Canterbury, Richard Bancroft, expelled Puritan ministers.

Towards the end of James' reign, a struggle developed within the Church between the 'High Church' party, led by Archbishop Laud and supported by both James and his successor Charles I, and the Calvin-inspired Protestants among the gentry in the House of Commons. There were other both long- and short-term causes of the Civil War, but some of the seeds of that war were already sown in what became both a religious issue and a struggle for supremacy between King and Parliament. Charles I, who came to the throne in 1625, continued his father's tolerant attitude towards religion, not least because of the Catholicism of his French wife, Henrietta Maria.

Donne made the move from Catholicism to the Anglican Church; George Herbert was fortunate in facing no such crisis. By birth, belief, and probably temperament, he was and remained a member of the Established Church, and his position within that Church is made clear by the fact that it was Laud himself, not yet Archbishop, who persuaded him to take the living at Bemerton where he spent the last three years of his life. However, religious diatribe and division have no place in Herbert's poetry, but only a loving devotion which is at the heart of his own faith and life. Herbert was perhaps fortunate in that he did not live to see the bitterness of Laud's later years, when his persecution of the Puritans (the result of which may be seen in that song of hopeful, faithful exile, Marvell's 'Bermudas') and violent attacks on all who did not precisely share his views on liturgy and ritual helped to bring about his impeachment and, in 1645, his death. To be fair to Laud, he had carried out many necessary Church reforms, increased the Church's wealth and prestige, encouraged scholarship within the Church and approved the arts, especially the Church music loved by Herbert and Vaughan.

Unfortunately, by the outbreak of Civil War in 1642, drama and poetry were seen as immoral by many Puritans, and the principal reading was religious treatises and tracts, and numerous volumes of sermons. The term 'Puritan' is useful but ambiguous, in that it covers a wide range of religious thought, including Anglicans who had particular scruples about, for example, vestments (the liturgical garments worn by the priest in cele-brating the Mass), and the mainly Calvin-inspired groups such as the Presbyterians, as well as individualists like John Milton, who cannot easily be put under any label.

Early in the Civil War, Parliament banned the Prayer Book, took action against Anglican worship and forbade the celebration of the major religious festivals such as Christmas. Oliver Cromwell (Parliamentarian leader and Protector under the Commonwealth) suppressed the most liberal and democratically-inclined of the sects, the Levellers, and allowed Parliament to be purged of the moderates. In 1649, to the horror of both Catholic and Protestant Europe, Charles I was beheaded. The monarchy was abolished, and Cromwell moved north to attack Scotland, which was threatening to have Charles II crowned. However, the Commander-in-Chief of the army, Thomas Fairfax, refused to extend bloodshed to Scotland and retired to his country estate in Yorkshire. Fairfax had opposed the execution of Charles I, and was essentially a man of peace and justice. He settled back into country life and the cultivation of his gardens, which were such a source of inspiration to his daughter's tutor, Andrew Marvell.

The background of Marvell's youth, then, was the Civil War, although it is likely that he was abroad for much of the war itself. Like Fairfax, by whom he was probably strongly influenced, he disliked the execution of Charles I, and had a deep hatred of civil war. Marvell's next appointment took him to the house of John Oxenbridge at Eton, as tutor to Cromwell's ward William Dutton. Oxenbridge was a Puritan who had spent time in Bermuda as an exile, but although some influence on Marvell is certain, Marvell seems to have maintained friendships with liberal Anglicans such as John Hales; the balance and fair-mindedness of his nature made it difficult for him to be as extreme as his masters. He genuinely mourned the death of Cromwell; he served as Member of Parliament for Hull under Charles II; he reserved the right to be critical of both.

Marvell was an active politician as well as a poet, and religious faith is less central to his writing than it is in the poems of the later Donne, Herbert or Vaughan. We may turn this round to say that he was a poet as well as a politician in an age of religious and political controversy, and therein lies the danger of seeing these poets only in terms of their religious background. Of course they were influenced by the turbulent times in which they lived, and by the centrality of religion mentioned at the start of this chapter. But they were not ordinary men: they were gifted, imaginative, creative, and so perhaps more prone to a sensitive and generous view of human nature than most. If it is necessary to see them in context, it is important also to remember Donne's picture of Truth, sitting on top of a craggy hill, to be reached only with difficulty and with integrity.

Belief

Within the writing of all four poets, there are frequent references to particular ideas and doctrines, some of especial interest to their contemporaries and some which have remained constant in Christian belief to the present day. To non-Christians, such terms may present a barrier to the understanding and appreciation of the poetry, and so they are now defined, not as a theologian would define them, but as far as possible in terms of the ordinary faith of the seventeenth century, allowing for the wide differences of interpretation described above. The references to individual poems are examples of the use of the terms discussed, and not in any way a comprehensive list.

Central to all Christian belief, then as now, is the Person of God, known to believers as the *Holy Trinity* (Donne's 'Three person'd God', 'Holy Sonnet xiv'). The three Persons are God the Father (Creator), God the Son (Jesus Christ) and God the Holy Spirit (the Being of God Who is present within the believer); the Three Persons form One God (as Donne's poem clearly shows). It is impossible (even for theologians!) to define the Trinity totally, as God must by His own nature be beyond the compass of the human mind. The simple description just given is enough for the understanding of the poetry.

The *Bible* is the inspired word of God, which is not to say that it is to be believed literally, although historically most Christians probably have taken it literally before the development of a modern critical approach to all literature. In the first part of the Bible, the Old Testament, we read of the *creation* of the world by God out of what the Bible calls the 'void', which is 'nothingness'; in Metaphysical poetry this is often referred to as 'chaos', the absence of order. In the 'Nocturnall', Donne thinks of the lovers as 'two Chaoses' when they thought of anything other than their love; order was no longer in their lives. (We may compare Othello, declaring to Desdemona:

> . . . when I love thee not,
> Chaos is come again.

The play was probably written at about the same time as Donne's poem, or a little earlier.)

In the creation of man, the Bible declares that God breathed the breath of life and 'man became a living soul'. It is difficult to define the word '*soul*', although we probably know instinctively what is meant: it is that essential part of the human being which is not material and yet is associated with the individual personality, and which survives after death. In 'The Funerall', Donne sees the soul as that part of himself which has gone to heaven (leaving the external soul, the hair of his mistress, in control of his body). Although that poem is light-heartedly cynical, he writes in 'The Extasie' of the union of the lovers' souls, a spiritual union which precedes physical union. Donne in general follows the teaching of Aristotle which was adopted by the Church, seeing the soul as co-existent with the body and continuing after death. Vaughan tends to follow the Platonic idea of the soul pre-existing the body, as the pure being which temporarily inhabits the body during the period of earthly existence. (This point is further dealt with in the Commentaries on 'The Extasie' and Vaughan's 'The Retreate'.)

The beings created by God are given the names *Adam and Eve*, the first man and woman. They are created in the image of God and intended for eternal fellowship with Him. *Paradise* (the Garden of Eden) was their natural home, and entirely at their disposal except for one fruit (usually thought of as an apple) which God had forbidden them to eat. Satan (the

Devil), in the shape of a serpent, tempted Eve to eat the apple by telling her that she would not die but would be 'like God'. She ate, persuaded Adam to eat also, and both were thrown out of Paradise to live a human existence including pain and limited by death. By this *Fall*, all mankind shares the tendency to sin ('original sin') and is in a sense guilty with Adam.

Modern Christians usually see this story as a myth which teaches that man is created by God and intended for eternal life with Him, but that unbelief and pride (the temptations of the serpent) always lead man away from God in an imperfect world. To educated people in the seventeenth century, both versions were probably acceptable. They believed in a literal Adam and Eve and could even 'place' Paradise (in his 'Hymne to God my God', Donne refers to the belief that Paradise and Calvary – the place of Christ's crucifixion – were in the same spot). At the same time, they saw the story as an allegory of man's temptation and fall into sin, and so were able to universalise it. It becomes a powerful symbol for evil in the lives of men. Donne uses the story, assuming no doubt rightly that his readers would understand the significance of it, in 'Twicknam Garden': the garden might have been like Paradise, but he has brought his own serpent with him in his bitter anger, which will prevent his receiving solace ('such balmes') from his surroundings. He accepts the doctrine of original sin in himself, in his 'Hymne to God the Father':

> . . .that sinne where I begunne,
> Which is my sin, though it were done before. . .

Herbert omits the detail of the story, but uses it powerfully as a symbol of fallen man in 'Easter Wings', contrasting the Fall with Christ's Resurrection.

The Reformation, as we saw earlier in this chapter, involved not only religious attitudes and political thinking, but also fundamental differences in doctrine. Original sin might be accepted by both Catholic and Protestant, but the answer to sin was very different. The key words are 'predestination' and 'grace'. John Calvin (1509-64) was the fiercest and most influential proponent of the doctrine of *predestination*. By this, he meant that because of original sin, all men were sinners, but God chose those whom He willed to be saved; in Calvin's own words:

> . . .all are not created in equal condition; rather, eternal life is fore-
> ordained for some, eternal damnation for others.

Nothing that a human being could do would change God's decision; God's will is supreme, and by His own nature must be right. The certainty of their own salvation and of the damnation of others caused intolerance and persecution by extreme Calvinist Protestants in the same way that they had been persecuted by the Roman Catholic Church. In England, and within the Church of England, this extreme view was held but was never accepted by all, and was strongly opposed by many, such as Archbishop Laud.

George Herbert himself probably gives the clearest and most attractive picture of 'grace'. While not denying original sin, he puts the emphasis on the love of God for all His creatures, however unworthy (see especially his poem, 'Love'), and in particular on the expression of that love as grace, which can be roughly defined as the love of God taking the initiative in man's salvation; all that is needed from man is the response of faith. The 'silk twist let down from heaven' in 'The Pearl' is this grace, and the poet is guided and taught by God in his climb to heaven. The initiative is clearly God's, and there is no suggestion that the rope is not there for all men. Indeed, Herbert's parable-sonnet, 'Redemption', shows this: the title literally means the buying back of a slave in order to give him his freedom. The tenant in the story does no more than look for his Lord; the suit is granted at once. The sinner is free from his sins because of the grace of God. This is Donne's sure hope when he is assailed by despair: 'Thy Grace may wing me to prevent his art. . .' ('Holy Sonnet i').

The Metaphysical poets use not only doctrine in their writing, but also *Old Testament* stories. These stories, like that of the Fall, were certainly believed literally and probably also allegorically in the seventeenth century. Noah, best known for building an ark and so surviving the Flood (with which God destroyed the world except for the faithful family of Noah), had three sons, Shem, Ham and Japheth. Among these, the known world was rather oddly divided: Donne uses the general belief that Shem acquired what we now call Asia, while Ham got Africa and Japheth, Europe. The point Donne makes is that to reach the ends of the world the traveller must pass through narrow straits ('Hymne to God my God', ll. 19-20). The names are spelt in an unusual way. Donne's use of 'manna' is more interesting and complex, and will be discussed with the elements of the Mass, below. In general, the poets use Old Testament stories as common ground between themselves and their readers, and therefore as a useful source of imagery. There is nothing artificial in such use to men who had studied theology as an academic exercise, or, more usually, had read and discussed the Bible, its meaning and interpretation, from their childhood. If Vaughan incorporates the words of the Bible almost verbatim in his poetry (for example in 'Man', ll. 12-14) it is because biblical language is in a real sense also his own.

The *New Testament*, the second part of the Bible, being principally the *life and teaching of Christ*, is of more immediate impact, providing material not only for faith but also for meditation and example. The *Incarnation* (the teaching that Christ is God's Son, Who came to earth at a particular point in history to redeem fallen human beings) is scarcely touched on in Metaphysical poetry; the emphasis is strongly on the *Easter* story and its implications. The happenings of Easter are probably still fairly well known and may be summarised briefly. Christ's teaching and His miracles attracted crowds to Him and therefore became noticed by both Jewish and Roman authorities (the Romans were the occupying force in Palestine). The identification of Christ with the expected leader who was to save his people from Roman tyranny provided an excuse for the Jewish authorities to involve Roman authority to have Him arrested; the Jews themselves saw Him either as a nationalist leader or as a religious power, perhaps a prophet, who might threaten their position. Those who knew Him best understood, more or less, that His leadership was not a worldly one and that His message was universal; a few saw Him as the Son of God. After His arrest, Christ was crucified by the Roman authorities (acting under Jewish pressure); part of the execution involved the mockery of a crown of thorns and a purple robe (to both of which Donne refers in the last verse of the 'Hymne to God my God') and the 'title', King of the Jews. The cross, which was the instrument of execution, was set up on the hill of *Calvary*, outside Jerusalem. After His death, Christ's body was taken down and put in a rock tomb, which was sealed and guarded. On the third day after the crucifixion, the tomb was found open and the body gone; to the bewilderment and joy of His followers, Christ was seen alive, having risen from death to rejoin them. Later He ascended to heaven, to be again in glory with God the Father.

The Incarnation and this story of the Passion (suffering), death and Resurrection of Christ, and His subsequent Ascension, form the essential basis of Christianity, subject to re-interpretation in every age, but remaining as the foundation of faith. For the Metaphysical poets, such belief is central to their lives and their writing, and references to it abound. One of the most joyful is, of course, Herbert's 'Easter Wings', a celebration of the triumph of Christ over sin and death. It is also the basis of the same poet's 'Redemption', which shows not only the crucifixion but also its result, in the 'buying back' of man after his estrangement from God after the Fall.

To use the words 'buying back' is to oversimplify grossly the complex theology of the *redemption* of man. It may be summarised as God reconciling man to Himself by sending His Son into the world as a Man, and allowing human beings free will even to kill Him; the Son's willingness to accept death and to forgive not only His murderers but the sins of all mankind satisfies the demands of both justice (the penalty of sin is death) and mercy (the Son, who is not guilty, dies), and gives man a 'second chance' through acceptance of God's love, of the eternal life lost at the Fall. Thus Donne (after St Paul) refers to the 'first Adam' (who fell from Paradise) and the 'second Adam' (Christ, becoming Man in order to restore to all men the possibility of Paradise), ('Hymne to God my God', verse 5). In 'Holy Sonnet i', Donne associates the resurrection of Christ with his own redemption ('I rise again'), and in 'Holy Sonnet x', he declares that death itself is subject to Christ and has no permanent power over man ('death, thou shalt die'). The most moving picture of man's sin and Christ's redemption is Herbert's exquisite poem 'Love', with 'my shame' overcome by the One 'who bore the blame', the whole relationship being one of courtesy and intimacy, the love of the title.

Despair is not exactly a theological term, but it recurs in the analysis of Donne's 'Holy Sonnets' and in the 'Hymne to God the Father', and in a sense is born of the religious controversy in which Donne was brought up. It is likely that Donne's own nature made him tend to what the Elizabethans called 'melancholy', what we call 'depression'; the pressures put upon him in his attempts to win his own wife (he was briefly put in gaol for marrying her) and in trying to support her and their many children would easily have increased the depression to something close to despair. The horror with which Donne refers to this burden suggests that it was something worse than just a giving up of hope, however, and indeed from both Catholic and Protestant points of view, it was.

As a child, Donne would have been taught that despair was the ultimate sin, as the Roman Catholic Church provided an access to God for everyone, in the Mass. What is more, *only* the Roman Church provided this security, and therefore Donne as a Catholic would have found the idea of despair terrifying. Yet he had left the Roman Catholic Church and therefore distanced himself irretrievably from the means of gaining eternal life, a cause indeed of despair. Within his new Church (although not in the part of it to which he belonged) were those who held, with Calvin, that salvation is possible only to the elect, and Donne, very aware of his mis-spent youth, must have dreaded that if Calvin were right, he could hardly be among them. The fact that he did not accept Calvin's doctrine cannot have removed entirely from his mind the possibility of its truth. Caught by his past faith and guilt at his change, Donne must have been especially prey to and afraid of despair, and in his 'Holy Sonnets' (especially i, vii and xiv) we feel a sense of panic at the possibility; only in the 'Hymne to God the Father' does he expressly show God that 'sinne of feare' and find such assurance of God's mercy that he will 'feare no more'.

Two essential constituents of the life of the Church and of the individual Christian are referred to frequently in the poetry: prayer, and the Mass. *Prayer* is part of the two-way relationship of the Christian and God: it is a listening (which is close to meditation, sometimes called 'waiting upon God', a receptiveness on the part of the individual or of the corporate Church to the Holy Spirit). It is also a speaking, aloud or in silence, by which the individual or, again, the Church coming together, asks God for forgiveness, for guidance and for help for self or others. There are many forms of prayer, for instance Vaughan's 'Morning Watch', which is almost a prayer of adoration. Perhaps Vaughan's own definition of prayer within the same poem is the most simple and comprehensive: 'Prayer is the world in tune', a harmony between the responses of God and man.

The title of the poem suggests a *vigil*, which is prayer before a feast-day, usually a night spent in preparation. So Vaughan's awaking from sleep is preparation for a day and a lifetime in God's service, and he feels united (in harmony) with the whole universe. (The 'watches' of the night are divisions of the hours of duty, still used in a naval context.)

A religious vigil is usually preparation for a major festival, like Christmas or Easter, and therefore it has in it a hope and expectation of joy to come. In this sense, Donne's use of the word at the end of 'A Nocturnall' suggests a hope of resurrection for the poet and his dead love.

The Mass is the celebration of Christ's last earthly meal with His disciples before the crucifixion. At this meal, He took *bread* and *wine*, blessed them, broke the bread and distributed both bread and wine to His followers. As He did so, He called the bread 'my Body' and the wine 'my Blood', the bread, broken and distributed, and the wine symbolising the 'new covenant', the new relationship between man and God. The disciples were commanded to 'do this' (repeat Christ's actions) in remembrance of Him. The link with the breaking of Christ's body at the crucifixion and the spilling of His blood is obvious, and the Church has continued, according to Christ's command, to perform His actions and repeat His words, the bread and wine, known as the 'elements' of the Mass, being received by the faithful.

A good deal of the Reformation controversy rested upon the exact significance of the bread and wine, and Christians are still divided by this problem, although a wider interpretation by both Catholic and Protestant theologians has brought about much wider agreement than in the past.

In the seventeenth century, as now, Roman Catholics accepted the doctrine of *transubstantiation*, the belief that the bread and wine became literally (both spiritually and materially) the body and blood of Christ. To this, Protestants reacted strongly by denying any form of sacrifice, taking the actions to be a memorial and nothing more. The Church of England generally took a middle way, teaching that the bread and wine became spiritually but not literally Christ's body and blood (the doctrine known as 'real presence'). Interestingly, the 1552 Prayer Book effectively denied real presence, and Elizabeth I herself was probably responsible for the removal of this denial from the 1559 version; it was replaced in 1662 but changed to allow real presence but not transubstantiation. The more extreme Protestants continued to deny that anything more than a 'remembrance' was intended, and the Church of England probably contained adherents to most shades of opinion. Given this controversy, words which to the twentieth century appear remote and theological only, were frequently used in the ordinary discussions of educated people. So most would have heard the word 'transubstantiation' and would assume, more or less accurately, that they knew what it meant. Donne would certainly have been brought up to believe in transubstantiation, and probably (it would be impossible ever to be sure) was able to accept real presence as sufficiently close to his own belief. Herbert and Vaughan were likely to have believed in real presence; it is difficult again to be sure about Marvell's view, but he would be expected to follow the 'memorial' doctrine only, especially given the Puritanism of his clerical father.

Terminology has always followed schism: the word 'Mass' has been used in this book because it is the term most readily understood in a general way by non-Christians, espeically those of Christian background. It is the normal term of the Roman Catholic Church. Within the Anglican Church, the most common terms for the Sacrament are 'Holy Communion' or 'Eucharist', while Protestants, especially those furthest in doctrine from Catholicism, tend to use 'The Lord's Supper', referring to Christ's meal with His disciples (the 'Last Supper'), at which the Sacrament was instituted. None of these divisions is absolute, and many Christians will readily use different terms on different occasions.

References to what we will continue to call the Mass, for the reason given above, are frequent in the poetry, as we should expect. Herbert's 'The Collar' interweaves references to bread and wine as the poet suggests his rebellion against the altar which symbolises his faith (see the Commentary on this poem). The same poet's 'Love' uses the shared meal as a parable of his relationship with God, but the final lines ('taste my meat'. . . 'sit and eat') have Eucharistic overtones.

Donne's use of the Mass includes the link between *manna* and bread. In the Old Testament, the Israelites wandered through the wilderness for forty years; God led them and provided them with sustenance. When they were hungry and cried out for food, they were miraculously provided with manna, a white substance which fell with the dew and was collected each morning except the Sabbath (the day of rest); it melted in the hot sunshine of the day (as in Marvell's conceit of the dewdrop, the Christian soul, and manna, in the final lines of 'On a Drop of Dew'). As Christ spoke of Himself as 'the Bread of Life', and because of the use of the bread in the Mass as described above, manna became symbolic both of God's providing for His people and of the Mass itself.

The first verse of Donne's 'Twicknam Garden' gains in ferocity and in its ability to shock from an understanding of the rich overtones of his imagery. His 'spider love, which transubstantiates all' brings to the reader the significance of the Mass (God's loving sacrifice) and the depth of an anger which can turn even love to poison. The image is, of course, picked up in the reference to manna and also in 'loves wine' in the last verse. Donne is using words which he knew would not only be familiar to his readers, but would have the power to shock them profoundly. It is in a way a counterpart to the sexual imagery of 'Holy Sonnet xiv'.

Christian belief does not finish with Christ's Ascension into heaven; it looks forward to what is usually called *the Last Judgement*, the coming of Christ in glory to judge the world. Few believers would want to suggest how or when this might happen, and most are aware of it only as a continuation beyond time of Christ's condemnation of sin and redeeming love for sinners. Donne has a wonderful vision of the Last Judgement in 'Holy Sonnet vii', asking only for time for his own repentance. In his 'Hymne to God my God', he is able to feel joy in his approaching death with the hope of redemption which becomes certainty at the end of the 'Hymne to God the Father'.

Those who die for their faith are *martyrs*, and material remains or objects closely associated with saints and martyrs are called *relics*. So in 'The Funerall', Donne suggests that as he is a martyr to love, his mistress's hair might become a relic and so an object of false worship.

There are, of course, other religious terms used by the Metaphysical poets, which have not been discussed in this chapter. The most common have been included and it has become clear that all the poets have biblical and other religious teaching and indeed language so deeply embedded in their lives that it is a natural part of their poetic expression. Their poetry ranges from the dialectics of Donne's 'Satyre iii' to the mystical beauty of Vaughan's 'Quickness', but in each case it is founded on the intimate personal relationship with God best described by Herbert:

Me thought I heard one calling, *Childe*:
And I reply'd, *My Lord*.

4 SELECTED POEMS:
SUMMARIES AND
COMMENTARIES

The four Metaphysical poets whose work is discussed in this book have given me joy and intellectual stimulus for many years, and I feel deeply indebted to them. In summarising a selection of their poems, I have tried to share the vividness and complexity of their writing with readers of this book, while keeping, I hope, a due humility. There are more layers of meaning than I can reasonably show in modern English, and the mysticism of Vaughan, for instance, transcends ordinary prose. If the summaries help readers to understand enough to catch the beauty and intellectual skill of the original poetry, that is sufficient justification for writing them.

4.1 JOHN DONNE

The Good-morrow

Summary
1. The poet wonders what he and his mistress did before they loved one another. Perhaps their experience was childlike, mere country pleasure inadequate for sophisticated people. Perhaps they slept, like the mythological seven sleepers [see Commentary]. However it was, apart from this love, all pleasures were mere fantasies; if the poet ever saw, desired and possessed any beauty, it was only a dream of his present love.

2. And now the lovers wake, gazing at one another not because of lack of trust, but because love limits enjoyment of any other sight than the beloved, and makes their room, small as it is, a universe. Others may go on voyages of discovery to find new worlds, or in making maps, identify more and more worlds; the lovers possess one world which is two, each being and possessing a whole.

3. Each sees his or her own face reflected in the eyes of the beloved, and their faces show the truth and sincerity of their hearts. Where could

there be two better hemispheres [halves of the world they make up together], without the cold of the north or the sunset of the west? In alchemy, as in contemporary medicine, a balanced proportion was needed for continued existence; if their loves are united, or if both love so equally that neither declines, death [the ending of that love] will be impossible.

Commentary

The themes of this poem were standard to many earlier poets; what is interesting is the dramatic life and vitality which Donne gives them, and the sense of unity in love, strong in much of his poetry. That life worth the name begins with falling in love, that previous loves seem only dreams, that the lovers, gazing into each other's eyes, are the whole world to one another: these ideas are far from original. Donne is not, however, making abstract statements, but holding a conversation with his beloved. What could be more colloquial and apparently casual than the opening line, 'I wonder, by my troth. . .', and when did such a small and insignificant word as 'did' carry such enormous stress? The previous line leads up to it, it is the first word of the line and is followed by a comma. A simple word, 'did', sums up the whole of the lovers' past lives.

Donne then looks more closely at the past. It was spent accepting, as a baby at the breast, whatever it received with indiscriminate, naïve enjoyment. Indeed, it was as simple as the life of the country – usually disregarded if not despised by men in society or at Court. The poet's choice of words is interesting: 'weaned', 'sucked', 'childishly', 'snorted'. Nothing could be further removed from 'poetic diction'. These are ordinary homely words, at least two of them sounding vividly like their meaning. The transition from the homely to the wider comment comes by way of the 'seven sleepers' reference, the story of seven young Christian men who, persecuted by the Emperor Decius in AD249, took refuge in a cave and slept miraculously for 187 years.

From 'But this. . .', the verse becomes lyrical and flowing, echoing earlier love poetry, but Donne's realism again adds a new dimension. Previous beauty has not simply been admired from afar, but 'desired and got': a sudden and perhaps rather tactless honesty.

Nevertheless, the second verse makes it clear that this love is mutual and deeply trusting. The poet exults in his passion, looking to the contemporary outside world only to dismiss it. What price the voyages of discovery, when their two hemispheres make up one whole world? Each lover *is* a world, and each *has* the world of the other, a vision of duality existing alongside unity which is perhaps appealing to the modern reader. The imagery moves from the hemispheres to the compound of exactly equal ingredients which cannot be dissolved (and the necessary balance of elements in the human body); it seems to have come a long way from the 'I wonder, by my troth' of the beginning, for the poet has moved from conversation with his beloved to an analysis of the need for equality in love to an awareness of that equality as the basis for continuing love. The world to which the lovers waken may change and decay, but the quality of their love ensures that it will not. They will still share the wonder at whatever they *did*, before they loved.

The Sunne Rising

Summary
1. The sun is an old, undisciplined fool, prying on the lovers as if they heeded him. Other people, such as boys late for school or unwilling apprentices going to work, might need the sun; indeed, those who choose to ride early, hunting with the King in order to harvest favours, as ants in the countryside harvest food, might need to be called, but love is unchanging and unaware of time.

2. Why should the sun feel that he is so respected and successful? His rays could be shut out by a blink of the eyes if the lover could bear to shut out also the sight of his beloved. If the sun has not himself been blinded by her eyes, he should report whether all the wealth of the West Indies and spices of the East Indies are in their usual places, or whether, like majesty itself, they lie in bed with the poet.

3. She is all kingdoms and he is the ruler. Nothing else is reality. Princes only act the part of the lovers, honour is but pretence and wealth glittering emptiness, in comparison with the union of the lovers. The contraction of the 'real' world into the 'world' of the lovers makes the sun at least half as happy as they are, for he is old and will find it easier to warm so shrunken a space. If he shines on them, he indeed shines everywhere, for their room is the universe.

Commentary
Although the date of this poem is not known for certain, it must have been written after 1603, when King James I came to the English throne. James was renowned for his love of stag hunting.

'The Sunne Rising' is a poem of joyous, fulfilled love. The poet can hardly contain his sense of a pleasure so great that he can challenge the sun and the universe itself: he and his beloved cannot be subject to the mere laws of nature. Nevertheless, the poem contains a paradox often found in Donne's love poetry. Nothing exists apart from the experience of love, and yet the poet has a lively and humorous sense of the outside world and a sardonic approach to those whose interest is not love, but ambition. Court-huntsmen are courtiers who hunt with the King (and hunt Court favours), like hosts of ants off to the harvest fields (to 'harvest' the offices which are in the King's gift). The compression of imagery and the double meaning are typical of Donne. Outstandingly, this is a poem of conversation and wild, joyful hyperbole.

The poem's explosive beginning (Donne is fond of the forceful 'b' sound) sets the conversational tone. The sun is vigorously attacked as both a fool and a kind of 'peeping Tom', peering not only through the windows but even through the curtains. In spite of the poet's assertion that the lovers alone are reality, he is well aware of the world of late schoolboys and sour-faced apprentices: the sun is like a cross master, interfering and pedantic.

Both words and rhythm are close to those of ordinary speech. The energy and attack of the start develop into a longer line with repeated (and therefore emphasised) accusations of prying. We can hear the cynical amusement in the comparison between the flatterers round the King and ants hurrying off in search of their own harvest, and also the triumphant ring of the last two lines, with their assertion of the supremacy of love over time. The idea that time controls all human activity is both familiar and frightening to the Metaphysical poets; here, Donne turns it upside down.

The atmosphere of living conversation is also apparent in the carefully-emphasised 'tomorrow lāte'; the sun has arrived too early for the lovers on this occasion, and should behave better in the future. Many of Donne's favourite techniques can be seen in 'The Sunne Rising', from the dramatic beginning to his liking for lists (hours, days, months), from a variety of imagery (time divided into mere scraps, the awareness of distant riches newly discovered, astronomy) to the pun on 'hear' and 'here' in l. 20. At the end of the poem, Donne describes the lovers' bed as the centre of the universe and the walls of the room as the circle of the sun's movement. He is using the old Ptolemaic system of astronomy, in which the sun and the planets make concentric circles (spheres) around the earth. Almost certainly he did not believe this, but it would be sufficiently familiar to his readers to make a successful image.

Above all, the poet's ecstatic happiness is expressed in wild exaggeration to the point of self-mockery. The riches of the Indies, Kings, Princes, honour and wealth are brushed aside in the incredible assertion that 'nothing else is'. The comment that the sun is old and in need of an easy routine is cheeky and cheerful, and the pace is that of colloquial, vigorous speech with varying stress patterns and speed. The effect is always of friends conversing in a jovial, joking way, but the relaxed atmosphere comes of great technical skill, and its effect is to heighten the reader's awareness of a genuine and delightful happiness in love.

Song

Summary

1. The poet leaves his beloved not because he has wearied of her, nor because he expects to find any better love, but in order to help her to accept his ultimate, inevitable death by a jesting, 'pretended' death, which is his absence.

2. The sun on the previous day and has still reappeared in spite of having

no feelings on the matter and a much longer journey than the poet's. She should not, therefore, fear his departure, for he will travel faster and with much more urgency.

3. Human beings are so weak that while they cannot prolong happiness or recall happiness lost, they will work at ill fortune, prolonging the endurance and the suffering so that it overwhelms them.

4. Her sighs will dissipate his soul; her tears, well-meaning but cruel in their effect, will wash away his life blood. She cannot love him as she says she does, if in washing away her life, which is the best part of his, she also destroys him.

5. She must not look into the future fearfully, imagining ills which might befall him, or Fate may take up her prophecies and fulfil them. Rather, she should imagine that the lovers are merely turning aside in bed in order to sleep. Those who are necessary to each other's existence cannot truly be parted.

Commentary

Gentleness of tone and simplicity of lyrical movement are not often associated with Donne, but this poem, possibly intended to be set to music, reveals both. It may have been written for his wife when he left to travel the Continent in 1611; certainly the love it reveals is a quiet, deep, constant and mutual love such as his troubled spirit perhaps found in his marriage.

The rhythm is graceful and flowing, regular in pattern except for the few lines in which the poet wants to stress human efforts at creating discord (ll. 21–4); the awkward, jarring rhythm here stresses the meaning and contrasts strongly with the rest of the poem. The rhyme scheme is also regular, although the pattern changes within the verse (*abab*, *cddc*) so that it emphasises the lyrical flow without monotony.

Perhaps the tone is the most striking aspect. The poem appears simple, but there is considerable complexity of thought within its apparent simplicity; all is contained within the framework of gentle comfort and encouragement. The poet begins by asserting the constancy of his love, then gently shows the inevitability of the lovers' final parting. As if afraid to upset her further, he then writes quickly and lightly of the sun's laborious journey and the contrasting speed with which *he* will return. All readers can immediately identify with Donne's problem of human nature: the good is swiftly gone, the painful seems to last for ever.

Drawing on the popular belief that sighing and weeping undermine the sufferer's hold on life, Donne gently teases his wife with not really wanting to preserve him, but the verse ends with the beauty and simplicity of the six one-syllable words: 'Thou art the best of me'. Briefly, he touches on the danger of tempting fate, but, perhaps again afraid of causing her more distress, he ends with the simple, homely and intensely moving image of a separation which is no more than a brief turning aside: there is no parting

38

between those whose love is so deep. The movement of thought in this poem shows the usual agility of the poet's mind in a new guise, replacing energy and assertiveness with tender concern and consolation.

Twicknam Garden

Summary
1. Stricken by sighing and overwhelmed by tears, the poet comes to the garden to seek the fountain [new life]. His sight and hearing are open to healing influences which would be sufficient for any lesser pain. Yet he is a traitor to his own search for peace, as he brings with him a poisoned love which can turn even God-given bread to bitterness. In order that the garden may seem a true Paradise, he has brought his own destructive 'serpent' with him [his own bitter anger].

2. It would be better for him if winter darkened the beauty of the garden and a heavy [deadly] frost forbade the trees to mock him by flourishing. As he can neither endure his disgrace nor stop loving, he should be made by love into a piece of the garden, without feeling, or into a mandrake groaning in pain, or a stone fountain eternally weeping.

3. To such a fountain lovers should come with tear-vessels [lachry-matories] to catch the drops, tears which are the wine of true love, to use them as a test of their mistresses' tears at home. All that do not taste like his are false. It is not possible to judge a woman's thought from her tears any more than what she wears from the appearance of her shadow. Womankind is indeed contrary, for none is true except this one, who is faithful [presumably to her husband] only because that faithfulness is death to the poet.

Commentary
The bitterness of unrequited (or at least unconsummated) love is the theme of this poem, as vigorous in its anger and frustration as others of Donne's love poems are in their happiness.

We do not know who the 'she' of the poem is: perhaps Lucy, Countess of Bedford, whose estates included Twicknam Garden. It does not matter. Donne reveals an intensity of bitterness which sweeps the reader along in its emotional force, and at the same time expresses in complex imagery an intellectual analysis of his position. It is usually assumed that the 'disgrace' of which the poet speaks is the shame of loving a woman faithful to her husband, but this is only surmise from the contents of the poem. The violence is extreme in the first verse, although by the end we may feel that passion is a little abated, the immediate and personal agony being trans-muted into a general curse on womankind.

We recognise Donne's familiar energy, the emphatic 'b' sound as emo-tion bursts forth, the conversational tone, the varied speech rhythms, and 'shock' tactics. The poem is an intellectual analysis of the effects of unrequited love, and the intellect is always in control, but the reader is shaken by the intensity of emotion poured out with a passion at times both vicious and desperate. The compressed, rapidly-moving imagery suggests violent emotion, as it so often does in Shakespeare, also revealed is Donne's readiness to use theological concepts in an overtly sexual poem. The images, like the many run-on lines, interweave and overlap.

This complexity of thought process and compressed imagery is nowhere clearer than in the last five lines of the first verse. The poet is a 'selfe traytor' because he brings to the garden his own poison (as Satan brought death to Paradise), so that the 'balm' of the garden is useless. The idea of treachery leading to death immediately produces the 'spider' image, shocking in its application to love. Spiders were popularly supposed to poison all they ate, and Donne concentrates the venom of his bitterness in the two words 'spider love'.

This in itself is a horrifying juxtaposition of ideas, but the poet then moves instantly from human love to the remembrance of divine love in the Mass, to the transformation of the bread (in the next line associated with manna) to the Body of Christ (by implication associated with bitter gall). The central act of the Mass is thus identified not, as normally, with a miracle of divine love, but with a kind of reverse miracle, the transformation of love to poison (thus linked with the spider image). The garden now becomes the Garden of Eden (Paradise), ratified by the presence of the serpent, which the poet himself has introduced.

The imagery of the Mass is touched upon more lightly later in the poem, when Donne refers to his tears, 'loves wine', being the only valid test of love; the significance of 'loves wine' must be that of the wine of the Mass, but at this point in the poem the theological implications of the image are not pursued. Although the most complex imagery in the poem is religious (for a more detailed analysis of the symbolism, see Chapter 3), there is also the folklore image of the mandrake, a mythical plant with roots shaped like a man, which was supposed to shriek as if in pain if it was disturbed. More surprising is the simple, homely image of the shadow, which reveals the presence of the woman but not the fashion of her clothes.

The rapid transition of ideas and associations is controlled by an agile intellect; the movement of the poem is a progression of thought as well as of feeling, and both make powerful demands on the reader's mind and emotions. The paradox of 'truth killing' and the cynical surprise effect of the ending are in keeping with the energy and aggressiveness of the whole poem.

A Nocturnall Upon St Lucies Day, Being the shortest day

Summary

1. The poem begins [and ends] with St Lucy's Day, the midnight of the year, and at midnight itself [St Lucy's Day, December 13, was popu-

larly but mistakebly assumed to be the shortest day of the year]. The sun is exhausted, and can produce only flashes of light [the flasks are powder-horns] and no steady sunshine. As the sun has no power, so the world of nature seems bereft even of life-giving force; the earth, as if suffering from dropsy, has drunk all the dew which gives it life. So life is shrunk to the small space of a bed; it is dead and buried, but even this death can seem joyful in comparison to the poet, a mere memorial to life.

2. The poet is an example to future lovers, who have hope for the spring which seems to belong to another world. He is composed of all dead things; he has by the alchemy of love been brought to the pure essence of nothingness: the quintessence, the fifth stage of refinement, represents purity. His rebirth is formed only of negations ['things which are not'], as absence [loss of presence], darkness [absence of light] and death [loss of life].

3. Other lovers find their being from the positive aspects of life; they have souls, forms, spirit. The poet has been distilled to nothing [a limbeck is a distilling vessel], the container [grave] of all nothingness. In the past, he and his beloved would drown the world with tears, and the earth was without form when they showed any concern beyond their love; in absence, they were mere carcasses. [Separations of their bodies produced a soul, the source of life, which was no longer connected to their bodies; the souls remained together and the bodies were mere carcasses. Cf. 'The Extasie'.]

4. But through her death [which diminishes her being and therefore wrongs her], the poet has degenerated to the purest essence [elixir] of primeval chaos [the original 'nothing' before the creation]. If he were a man, then *ipso facto* he must know he is one; if he were a beast, he would have some powers of response. Even the plants or stones have some powers of attraction and repulsion. Everything has some property, but he is less than a shadow, which is at least caused by light and material substance.

5. He is nothing, without hope of a renewal of life. Other lovers who follow the lesser [real] sun will find that it enters the sign of Capricorn [the goat, representing lust], renewing their sexual desire so that their summer will be full of pleasure. Her festival [the beloved, the poet's sun, St Lucy, who are all associated with death] is the long winter's night and the poet prepares to meet her, knowing only the deep midnight of the year and of the day. [There is perhaps a tiny glimmer of hope at the end of the poem, a 'vigil' being a religious watch before a celebration [see Chapter 3]. The poet glimpses the hope of a resurrection for both himself and the beloved, even in the darkness of his soul.]

Commentary

This magnificent poem tells of the poet's grief at the death of his beloved. It is, as so often with Donne, difficult to know whether the experience was an immediate one, occasioned either by the serious illness or death of his patroness, Lucy, Countess of Bedford, or possibly by the death of his wife, or whether he has given a dramatic urgency to an accumulation of experience. Whatever the direct inspiration for the poem, Donne has given the sense of total loss both intellectual definition and emotional intensity. Rhythm, imagery, rhyme and choice of words combine to produce one of the most moving expressions in the English language of the death of the very soul in the experience of bereavement.

The poem begins quietly, with heavy stresses, slow movement and repetition which produce a sense of deep melancholy. The stress patterns are important in building up to a 'climax' word, as in the case of 'Lucies', isolated by punctuation and by its position at the beginning of the line, and carrying the emphasis of the paradox: 'Lucy' means 'light'. Heavily stressed lines such as:

> The worlds whole sap is sunke

or

> For I am every dead thing

echo the tolling bell and slow down the movement to a funeral pace.

Donne is at the same time skilful in varying the pace: the run-up of short syllables:

> . . . yet all these seem to laugh

to the surprise word 'laugh' make a sudden rapid movement caught back by the weight of the following line:

> Compar'd with me . . .

Similarly, the increase in tempo of 'you who shall be' ends in the heavy 'next world'. The most notable example of this change of pace occurs in the last verse, with the run-on lines from 'for whose sake' to 'new lust', followed by a return to the slow, melancholy rhythm of the beginning of the poem. This climax is stressed by the cumulative effect of the three rhymes, 'all', 'festivall' and 'call', and the concluding rhyming couplet.

We can see how important the rhythm of Donne's poetry is, and how the effect of the meticulous punctuation adds to the carefully controlled movement, the pauses being an integral part of the pattern. The effect, for instance, of the comma in the middle of 'Of all, that's nothing', followed by the even longer pause at the full stop, added to the slow movement of long vowel sounds ('o' as in 'oft', 'ow' as in 'grow'), is to produce an oppressive hopelessness which is inextricably linked to the poem's theme. The poet has descended the hierarchy of being: man-beasts-plants-stones- a mere image. He has become the lowest of all.

The imagery of 'A Nocturnall' shows Donne's normal range: alchemy, warfare, folklore (the beds-feet: the Elizabethans believed that the soul of the dying hovered at the foot of the bed), religion, astrology and the homely shadow. The poem is, of course, circular in movement, beginning with the midwinter festival of St Lucy followed by the poet's awareness that for other people, life and love continue, and ending with the repetition of that awareness followed by the midwinter midnight of St Lucy's Day. The end is quiet and lyrical, again echoing the beginning. The poem should be read aloud, so that the music of its sounds may be heard complementing the sad beauty of its words.

A Valediction: forbidding mourning

Summary

1. As good men die so peacefully that even their friends cannot be sure of the moment of death,

2. So the lovers should part, without floods of tears or tempests of sighs, for it would be profanity to publish their love to the world.

3. An earthquake causes damage and makes men fearfully consider its impact and significance, but the trembling of the heavenly spheres, far greater in movement, causes neither hurt nor fear.

4. Dull, ordinary lovers, whose love is based on their senses, cannot allow parting, because it would destroy the elements which make up their love.

5. The love shared by the poet and his beloved is so pure that they can hardly understand its quality. Their minds are mutually secure, and they are therefore less concerned that they are physically parted.

6. Their two souls, being united, are not divided by his departure; rather, they expand as beaten gold spreads rather than breaks.

7. In so far as the souls remain two, they are like the feet of a pair of compasses: she is firmly fixed, not seeming to move unless by the force of the other, moving foot.

8. Though she remains so fixed, she will lean and yearn after him, returning to her natural position only as he returns to her.

9. So, like the unmoving foot of the compasses is she to him, who must incline away from her. Her very steadfastness ensures that his circle is true and that he will complete his journey.

Commentary

This poem is best known for its famous image of the lovers as a pair of compasses, an image which is often treated as the most extreme example of Metaphysical wit (see Chapter 1) and as an illustration of the eccentricity of Donne's imagination. In fact, the poem contains a series of images culminating logically in this one, and it is not original to Donne, being used by earlier Italian poets and possibly reaching him by way of a sixteenth-century madrigal.

As so often in Donne's imagery, the progression is a development of the thought, not mere decoration of the emotion. The initial image is the quiet, homely comparison of the death of a good man with the parting of the lovers. Having established that such a parting must be, by the nature of their love, unnoticed by the rest of the world, Donne proceeds by a series of illustrations to analyse why this should be so: all nature obeys the law that the most violent movement is less disturbing than the more local and ostentatious. So the movement of the spheres, by which the heavenly bodies move in concentric circles round the earth, is universal and yet unobserved by man. Donne's next comparison looks more closely at the nature of love. 'Sublunary' lovers (ruled by the inconstant moon) depend on physical contact, while those whose love is refined can be compared to gold, beaten out into gold leaf, of a fineness and delicacy which seems hardly to be made of earthly matter. Such love is described in the lovely, melodious word 'inter-assured' ('assured' is three syllables); it cares less (the words are used in their original sense rather than in the weak modern form 'careless') for physical than for spiritual union.

It is at this point of Donne's analysis that we meet the compasses image. The comparison is stated, as it had been in the past, but it is also developed logically. This love which is like fine gold also allows the souls of the lovers to follow one another's movements without physical uprooting, the moving foot being dependent for its security on the steadfastness of the stationary foot, and the stationary foot being guided in its direction by the moving foot. Again, the interdependence of the lovers is emphasised as it had been by 'inter-assured', but the thought is now more complex.

There is one more development. The compasses, assuming that both are true, will describe a circle, perfecting their movement in the symbol of infinity and eternity (the circle is the equivalent of the wedding ring). The poet has thus proved that the complete, perfect love has no need of outward show. The floods of tears and tempests of sighs which were stock in trade of earlier poets have become not merely irrelevant but a denial of the true nature of love.

The verse form of this poem echoes its theme. The rhyme is regular throughout, and the rhythm, while allowing for the variations of speech emphasis common in Donne's poetry, maintains four stresses in each line. The effect is unassuming and constant, ending indeed where it began.

The Extasie

Summary

ll. 1–20 The lovers sit together on a bank of violets. Their hands are

closely entwined, and they gaze deeply into each other's eyes.
As yet this is the totality of their physical union, and the reflec-
tions in their eyes are the entire product of their love. As in a
battle between equally-matched armies, the outcome is uncer-
tain, so between the lovers the souls act as mediators, moving
forward to enhance their position. During this negotiation, the
lovers lie as still as effigies on tombs.

ll. 21-8   There might be a bystander who is so purified by love that he
can, as a totally rational mind, understand the very language of
souls. If so, in spite of being unable to distinguish between
speakers so united in thought and word, he might nevertheless
take away a new, still purer refinement of love, and so depart
enhanced by his experience.

ll. 29-48   The state of ecstasy which the lovers are experiencing makes
them more aware of the true nature of their love. They understand that it is not merely sexual, and also that they had not
previously realised fully the complexity of its motives. Just as
all separate souls contain a mixture of different, unidentified
elements, so love takes these separate mixtures and mixes them
again, so that their constituent parts are inseparable. A single
violet, poor and weak in growth, colour and size, is strengthened
and multiplied when it is transplanted. In the same way, when
love interfuses two souls, it produces one stronger soul which
remedies the defects of each, being separate. So the lovers, com-
posing one new united soul, understand their own being, the
constituent parts of which their love is made, and the unchanging
quality of the soul.

ll. 49-60   Why, then, do the lovers refrain from physical union? This is
not the whole of their love; their souls are the controlling force,
their bodies only the vehicle of their union. Nevertheless, it was
through a physical meeting that they first knew each other, and
for that they should be grateful. Their bodies subordinated
themselves and their senses [to the union of the souls]. but cannot be considered worthless, rather like a mixture in which the
inferior is made more valuable by union with the superior. As
spiritual influences sometimes work through the medium of the
air, so the union of souls can come about through the union of
the bodies.

ll. 60-76   As body and soul are linked by the spirits produced by the
blood, agents needed to complete a human being [see Com-
mentary], so the pure souls of lovers must condescend to
ordinary faculties with which the senses are linked. If this is not
so, the power of the soul is imprisoned. The lovers must now
return to their bodies, so that weaker men may see a physical

manifestation of love, for while the mystery of love is in the soul, the book of learning is the body. If some lover, united in love as they are, has heard the debate which their souls have undertaken and in which they are agreed, he can continue to watch them and will find little change in the nature of their love when their souls have returned to their bodies.

Commentary

This complex, highly intellectual poem appears at first strange to modern eyes, both in its apparent logic-chopping about the nature of sexual love and in its wide variety of imagery, some of it fully justifying the term 'conceit'.

The title itself is not to be confused with the modern use of the word – it has nothing to do with a state of extreme happiness. Ecstasy was a theological term, signifying the separation of the soul from the body, and producing a highly charged spiritual intensity in which insight and awareness were given, above the normal understanding of the human mind. In this poem, the lovers enter such a state of ecstasy, and through it are able to analyse the development of their love, its motives and the balance of its physical and spiritual components; when the souls are reunited with the bodies, the lovers have gained a philosophical understanding of the nature of human love which will remain through its physical consummation.

Donne is using and analysing ideas current in intellectual debates of his time. The neo-Platonic school of philosophers saw love as pure and spiritual in essence, sullied by contamination with the physical. The Aristotelian school, on the other hand, saw soul and body as interdependent ('Soul and body . . . are not two distinct things, they are one thing presenting two distinct aspects.' R. D. Hicks, Introduction to Aristotle's *De Anima*). Donne clearly sides with Aristotle, but in 'The Extasie' he discusses the quality of that interdependence, the production of a new and strengthened soul when love 'interinanimates' (lovely word) two weaker and more fragile souls. This new soul is the dominant factor, the physical bodies being under its control, but Donne is careful not to devalue the body. It is the 'sphere', the manifestation of the abler soul, and without it that soul is imprisoned, unable to express itself fully.

The detail of the poem is often obscure to the modern reader. A heavenly body was believed to consist of a sphere (vehicle) and intelligence (controlling force): thus ll. 51-2. The influence of spiritual forces comes to man through a medium which is in itself less pure, the air (ll. 57-8). The union of body and soul makes up a man, as Donne explains in one of his sermons, but the blood produces spirits which 'are a kind of middle naure, between soul and body' (*Sermons XI*), and these spirits strive to achieve the purity of the soul in order to link the soul to the body (ll. 61-4). Such ideas are difficult, but Donne's major thesis, that the place of the physical is justified in love as it is interdependent with spiritual union, both receiving due respect, is one which seems, perhaps surprisingly, modern.

The range of imagery in the poem is also striking. The traditional pastoral setting, as used by earlier poets such as Sir Philip Sidney, has added significance. The bank of violets (flowers symbolic of faithful love) supports the lovers as would a pillow on a bed – and the sexual overtones are stressed in the adjective 'pregnant'. Best-known of all the poem's images is that of the lovers' eyes twisted on a double string like beads: it is exotic and witty, but the poet moves on swiftly to military strategy and the simple 'like sepulchrall statues' (slow because of the long vowel sounds and repeated 's', and suggestive of a stillness like death, the body without its soul). The references to alchemy and to the philosophy of love give way to the pastoral image, unusual in Donne's writing, of the violet transplanted. Astronomy, physiology, the imprisonment of a great Prince, and the book by which love is learnt, illustrate again the breadth of the poet's intellect and the agility of his mind, and the dramatic device of the silent onlooker, learning as the reader does from the lovers' experience, make this a poem of great skill and power. In its regular, unassuming rhythm and rhyme, it achieves the force of a philosophical debate; in its honest appraisal of the nature of human love, it is universal in theme.

The Funerall

Summary
1. Whoever comes to prepare the poet's body for burial must not disturb or ask questions about the fine bracelet of hair which adorns his arm. It is a holy symbol, representing his outer soul which, in the absence of the inner soul which has gone to heaven, is now in charge as Viceroy of his body and will keep it from decay.

2. For if the nerves, controlled by the brain, are linked through every part of his living body and so make him one being, how much more effectively will his dead body be preserved by the bracelet of hair which grew towards heaven and was formed with strength and skill by a better brain. But perhaps she merely intended that he should [by the bracelet] be kept conscious of his pain, as prisoners are handcuffed when they are condemned to death.

3. Whatever her exact meaning, the hair must be buried with the poet, for as he is a martyr to love, it might become a relic and encourage idolatry. As his humility before her was shown by his taking her hair as a symbol of his soul, so his pride will be satisfied in that, although she would save no part of him, he can take to the grave a part of her.

Commentary
'The Funerall' is characterised by two outstanding features: its vitality, shown in its direct, conversational approach, and its logic, carefully built up to the final half-bitter, half-cynical jest.

Vitality seems perhaps a strange word for a poem with such a title, and yet from the first line, addressed forcefully to the reader (one is tempted to say listener), through the rapid movement of varied line lengths and frequent run-on lines to the paradox of the punch line, there is a sense of aggressiveness and energy which carries the reader with it.

The twentieth century is conditioned to avoid the subject of death, and particularly the unpleasantness of physical decay, but such an attitude was unknown to the Jacobeans. Constant reminders of the proximity of death (severe plague years, the frequent deaths of women in childbirth and of children themselves) made it the subject of what seems to be morbid fascination; contemporary Jacobean playwrights such as John Webster spared no gory details of violent death in their writing. Donne is in this, as in so many things, a realist. A cynical, witty poem about the pain of unrequited love accepts the physical as well as the emotional consequences, and if these consequences include death, then the corruption of the body follows inevitably. Donne accepts the facts and enjoys getting his own back on the woman who has made him suffer.

Enjoyment comes strongly through the logical progression of the poem. Whether Donne was really suffering the after-effects of a painful love, or whether he was using the old theme of death-of-a-broken-heart and giving it a new twist, is immaterial. He sets out the conceit (see Chapter 1) of the efficacy of his mistress's hair as a secondary soul, and then develops the image. In the first verse, he is her subject (the 'Provinces' she controls); by the second verse, he is her prisoner, condemned to die; in the third verse, he has become a martyr to love, and martyrs have power over the living (their relics might become the focus of worship: see Chapter 3); now, from his position of strength, he can seek revenge by carrying at least a part of his tormentor to the grave with him. The ingenuity of the poem consists not only in its outline, but also in its detail. In the second verse, as the mistress's hair is superior in that it grew upward (and so towards heaven) and that it carried with it all her power and cunning (highly developed in her particular brain), it is *therefore* more efficacious in preventing his decay than his own brain and nervous system could have been. The logic is outrageous, as it is intended to be; the reader needs to share with the poet the enjoyment of such an outrage.

The poem is, of course, highly dramatic, almost a dialogue between the dead poet and the living mourner. Its movement is rapid through the first seven lines of each verse, although varied in the short and medium length lines. It gains momentum in the very short, little-stressed seventh in preparation for the very long eighth line. This is itself divided into two, the emphasis being strongly on the last few words; indeed, the last five short words of the poem carry four stresses: 'I bury some of you'. The holding back of the rhyme from the sixth line to the end of the extended eighth line adds to the tremendous attack, as the logic of the poet's position and the energy with which he reveals his triumph come together.

Satyre iii

Summary

ll. 1–15   Pity conflicts with anger; proud scorn forbids the poet to weep;

he can neither laugh at nor weep for sins if he is wise, and railing cannot cure long-standing maladies. Is not religion as worthy of the total devotion of our souls as virtue was for the pre-Christian age? Are not the joys of heaven strong enough to control desires, as earthly honour was strong enough for our ancestors? Alas, even if we have greater means to draw us to heaven, earlier men may prove more righteous in the end. Our parents, meeting ancient philosophers of the strict morality which was their faith, may hear in heaven that we who were taught easy and direct ways to follow, are damned.

ll. 15-28 If we fear, we should fear damnation, for such a fear is a sign of courage and high valour. Mankind has courage: men will fight with the Dutch [at the time, against the Spaniards], live in the wooden sepulchres of ships, prey to the rages of their commanders, to storms at sea, to fighting or to shortage. They will dive into the depths of the sea and explore the depths of the earth. They have courage hot enough to thaw the ice of a north-west passage. They will for mere monetary gain, like salamanders [which were reputed to live in fire] or like Shadrach, Meshach and Abednego thrown into the fiery furnace, bear the fires of the Spanish Inquisition and of equatorial heat, which melts our very bodies [a limbeck was a vessel used in distilling]. Must every man who will not call another's mistress a goddess defend himself with the sword or be forced to swallow insults?

ll. 28-42 This is mere courage or straw! Will a coward, who makes such a pretence of courage, yield to his own enemies and God's, the God Who put him as sentinel in a beleaguered world; will he leave the [moral] battlefield? Men should know their true enemies: the foul Devil, whom they try to please, would give them his whole kingdom, glad to be rid of it, but for hate, not love. The world is passing away, and worldliness, man's other foe, is coming to an end, and those who love the world love only a withered, worn strumpet. Most of all, men love the sins of the flesh [which bring death] and earthly pleasures; they hate their good souls, which allow their bodies to find true joy.

ll. 43-69 Seek true religion. But where is it to be found? The man of incense, finding true religions abandoned here [in Protestant England], seeks her at Rome - there, because that is where he knows she was a thousand years ago. He has the same respect for her, in rags, that we have here for the canopy over the throne where the prince sat yesterday. On the other hand, the continental Protestants [typified by the 'Germanic' name Crantz] will not follow such a colourful religion, but love only that which at Geneva [home of the Calvinists] is called religion, plain, simple, solemn, new, contemptuous of others but unlovely itself. So among those given to lechery, there is the type who thinks no woman attractive but a coarse country drudge. The Greek sort remains at home here; he is told by some preachers, who are no better than bawds selling their mistresses to further their own ambitions, supporting laws which are fashionable because new, that the religion which dwells here is the only perfect one. So he embraces her, whom his godfathers present to him in his weak youth, as wards in court take the wives their guardians offer or face paying a fine. The uncaring Phrygian [Phrygians worshipped a multiplicity of gods] abhors all because all cannot be good, just as a man who knows some women are whores will not dare to marry any. Gracchus [the liberally-minded man] loves all equally, thinking that as women in different countries wear different types of clothing and yet are all women, religion is the same. Such blindness produces an excess of light.

ll. 69–84 Unmoved by all this, man must of necessity choose one religion and only one, and it must be the true one. Ask your ancestors which is she, and let them ask theirs; although truth and falsehood are like twins, yet truth will be a little older. Strive earnestly to seek her, for, the poet is convinced, he who seeks the best is not a man of no religion or of the worst sort. To adore a holy image, or to scorn it, or to protest at it [i.e., to be a Roman Catholic, anti-Catholic or Protestant] may indeed all be bad. Doubt may be wisdom. On a strange road, it is not wandering to stop and ask the right direction; not bothering or running in the wrong way, clearly is. Truth stands at the top of a huge hill, cragged and steep, and he that will reach her must go this way and that and so overcome the steepness of the ascent. He must also strive to find truth before the twilight of death overcomes his soul, for in that night none can work.

ll. 85–99 To intend something suggests delay: take action now. Hard physical achievement causes pain to the body; so difficult knowledge will require great endeavour of the mind, and religious truth is as dazzling as the sun and yet plain for all to see. Keep to the truth when it is found; men are not so unfortunate that God has given kings a blank cheque to kill whomever they hate. They are not God's deputies, but merely hangmen serving fate. He is foolish and wretched who will allow his soul to be tied to the laws of man, by which it will not be tried at the Last Judgement. What then will it benefit him to say that Philip [King of Spain], or Gregory [Pope Gregory VII], Harry [Henry VIII] or Martin [Luther] taught him this? Is it not merely the excuse for contrary opinions, equally strongly held? Cannot both sides say the same?

ll.100-10 In order to obey power, the limits of that power must be
known. Once the limits are accepted, the nature and being of
power changes and then to submit to power is idolatry. Power is
truly like a stream. The flowers that dwell at the calm source of
a rough stream thrive and flourish. Those which leave their roots
and give themselves to the overwhelming force of the raging
stream, are driven through mill-races, rocks, woods, and at last,
almost destroyed, vanish into the sea. So it is with souls which
choose to have faith in the power unjustly claimed from God by
men, rather than to trust in God Himself.

[More detail about the religious ideas contained in this poem is found in
Chapter 3.]

Commentary

Donne wrote a series of satires on a variety of topical subjects, probably
during the 1590s. Satire was an established form, used by Horace, Juvenal
and Persius, and Donne was influenced by the Roman tradition of harsh
satirical writing, so much so that Pope 'tidied up' the satires a century
later, making them more smooth and lyrical.

They were intended to be harsh, and 'Satyre iii', which is the most
famous, deals with a serious contemporary problem particularly close to
Donne himself: in a time of many different forms of Christianity, how was
it possible to find which was true? The poem was probably written in the
early 1590s when Donne was still a Catholic, and certainly it comes down
on the side of historical truth rather than innovation. Nevertheless, it is a
courageous poem both personally and socially, both for its Catholic bias
and, perhaps even more, for its insistence on truth. Men were not to be
subject to the whims of a religious leader, be he King or Pope, but were to
look to the 'stream's calme head', God Himself, source of all earthly
power. At the Last Judgement, it will be an earnest search for God's truth
which will be counted righteous, and not blind obedience to the exigencies
of time.

At the heart of the poem is Donne's picture of Truth, difficult to reach
and making great demands on all who try. With a compassion and tolerance
unusual at the time, Donne shows that honest doubt and questioning are
never wrong: blind obedience or apathy always so. The movement of the
verse echoes the meaning, with the strong sense of physical effort in 'about
must, and about must goe'. The effect is harsh and disjointed, as a climber
would move in fits and starts, overcoming physical difficulties. The only
lines which could be called lyrical in movement are those beginning 'As
streames are, Power is', when, the mental conflict over, Donne can assert
the supremacy of the divine Will.

The imagery of 'Satyre iii' covers much of the range associated with
Donne's later poetry – voyages of discovery (and the realistic comment
about 'ships woodden Sepulchers'), biblical references, war, and the very

immediate image of the hill of Truth. Most of all, the images are sexual. The dying world is likened to an old strumpet, some lecherous men find only rough country girls attractive, some preachers are like ambitious bawds, some men do not dare to marry because some women are whores. These images are vivid and dramatic, and show the easy use of sexual references in religiously-inspired poetry which reappears much later in, for example, 'Holy Sonnet xiv'.

Donne uses the couplet form, rhyming regularly with five iambic feet to the line. However, the rhythmical patterns vary a good deal as the poet needs emphasis or wants to stress difficulty, so that the total effect is not of a flowing, dexterous verse form like that, for instance, of Pope. It is harsh and demanding, as befits a poem revealing something of the struggles of a young Elizabethan Catholic who wanted fame and fortune, but not at the expense of truth.

Holy Sonnets i, x, xiv

These three of Donne's Holy Sonnets have been chosen to illustrate different aspects of his religious writing. Exactly when they were written is not certain; most of his religious poems are assumed to belong to the period after the death of his wife in 1617, but some were probably written earlier.

Donne's need to explore and analyse is as clear in these poems as in the earlier secular writing, and his passionate, tormented nature does not change because he is now an ordained priest. Indeed, his sense of guilt and fear of ultimate despair sometimes make him more aggressive and demanding towards God than he had been towards women in his younger days. He had achieved within the Church the sort of popular esteem and influence at Court which he had fought for during many years, and was aware of temptations both to pride and, more frequently, to despair at his own unworthiness. The life he had led as a young man, in which he had influenced others, now seemed to him sinful and abhorrent, and yet the same restless energy and questioning spirit tormented him. Most of all, he had achieved his position, however belatedly, as a result of rejecting his Catholic upbringing and accepting the Anglican faith; he had to preach against Catholicism in strong terms (as in *Sermon I*, St Paul's Cathedral, Christmas Day, 1622). It cannot have been easy for one whose family had suffered for its faith and who had battled for years to come to terms with a different faith; it would be surprising if Donne had not had deep feelings of guilt and inadequacy. The death of his wife Ann undoubtedly added emotional insecurity to his other torments, and many of his religious poems cry out for a peace and a stability in faith which he found it difficult to attain.

The three sonnets chosen have been summarised consecutively, and the Commentary deals with each and with the links between them.

Summaries

Holy Sonnet i
God has made the poet, and can God's work simply decay? The poet needs rebuilding now, as he nears death: indeed, he seems to gather speed towards his oncoming death, and all the pleasures of life are in the past.

He dare not look around him, for despair is behind and death before, creating terror as his body is wasted by sin, weighing it down towards hell.

God alone is above, and when by God's grace the poet can look towards Him, he can rise again, but Satan so tempts him to despair that in his own strength he can scarcely sustain life. Grace must give him wings to forestall the Devil, and God like a magnet, with unyielding determination, must draw the iron of the poet's heart to Himself.

Holy Sonnet x
Death should not be boastful, although some have called him mighty and dreadful, which he is not. Many people whom death thinks he can overcome – and the poet includes himeslf – do not truly die. Much pleasure is to be found in rest and sleep, which are only images of death, and therefore much more must come from death itself. Some of the very best men go soonest to death, and find rest for their bodies and deliverance for their souls.

Death is the slave of many kinds of weapons, from fate and chance to war and sickness; opium or charms can produce even better sleep. Why then should death be so proud? After one short sleep comes eternal life, when there shall be no more death; death itself shall die.

Holy Sonnet xiv
God, the Holy Trinity, must batter at the heart of the poet. So far, God has tried gently to bring the poet to repentance, but if he is to stand before God, then God Himself must first strike him down, using all His force to destroy and remake the suppliant.

The poet is like a town conquered by an enemy, striving unsuccessfully to let in its original ruler, whose Viceroy, the power of reason, is a captive and has submitted.

Yet the poet truly loves God and wants God's love. He is like a woman betrothed to an enemy, who calls on her true lover to free her, take her to himself and make her his captive. Such a one, like the poet, will never achieve freedom unless he is captured (by God); he will never achieve purity unless he is overwhelmed (raped) by God.

Commentary
All three poems adhere to the sonnet form of fourteen lines divided into the octet (eight) and the sestet (six), with a turning point in meaning or emphasis between the two. Donne's rhyme scheme is unusual: *abba, abba, cdcdee* (the octet rhymes are different from Shakespeare's or Sidney's usual forms but similar to those of Petrarch; the sestet differs from Petrarch,

however); but he uses the turning point between octet and sestet in the normal way. Most English sonnets are essentially iambic (unstressed syllable followed by stressed); Donne keeps to this as his basic rhythmical pattern, but changes it frequently, forcing the words to obey his dramatic intention and heightened emotions. At times he uses heavy stress in order to emphasise the meaning of the words: '. . .to bréak, blówe, búrn and máke me ñew.) The explosive 'b' sound, of which Donne is so fond, is felt in thislist as at the start of the sonnet ('Batter my heart. . .'); it is the same dramatic technique found in 'The Sunne Rising' ('Busie old foole. . .') and produces the same sense of urgency in the reader. The same fondness for lists which has been noticed in the secular poems is shown here, not just in the emphatic example quoted above, but also in the diminishing of death, the slave to fate, chance, kings, and so on. Here the list has the opposite effect, that of accumulating the accidents to which death is subject, rather than giving emphasis to a hammer-blow series of actions.

The Holy Sonnets are intensely personal, and their dramatic effect is largely the result of the struggle which is worked out through their lines: in these poems, as in the earlier love poetry, the problem is thought through during the poem itself, rather than reflected on with hindsight. Much use is made of the personal pronoun, and at times there is a sense of sheer terror on the part of the writer. This is particularly true of the first of the three sonnets discussed. The poet is weighed down by the awareness of approaching death and by the closeness of despair (see Chapter 3, where the significance of despair and of grace is discussed more fully). The forcing of words into the confined space of a five-stress line (as at l. 8) suggests a rising panic. At the turn, the change of direction in the ninth line, hope reappears, with the double significance of 'only': God alone is above, only God Who is above. The hope cannot be in the poet's own strength, but in the grace of God. Theologically, the problem is resolved, but it is difficult to believe that emotionally the poet has reached any resolution of his fear.

Yet Donne does not always write from the abyss. 'Sonnet x' is a clarion call of hope, indeed of certainty, that death is always followed by resurrection. The opening statement is strong, and the emphasis on the small words 'thou art not so', each carrying stress, leads to the bold assertion that death can bring only pleasure. The turn in this case is from the attractiveness of death to its triviality; again there is a short list, ending with the long-vowelled line in which poppies or charms are equal in importance to death. Donne is a master of the final couplet: it is not a mere rounding-off of the sense, but a logical conclusion of the argument, and in this case it has a grandeur and a defiance which bring the sonnet to a triumphant end.

'Sonnet xiv' has neither the near-despair of the first nor the certain faith of the second of the poems considered. It is the most famous of the Holy Sonnets for its dramatic vitality and its startling imagery. The contrast of soft consonants and long vowels in 'breathe, shine and seeke. . .' (God's gentle treatment) with the harsh sounds, repeated explosive 'b', and short vowels in 'breake, blowe, burne. . .' emphasises again the poet's urgency, the demands with which he assaults God, the ferocity of his need. The paradox of 'that I may rise and stand, o'erthrow me' duplicates in its form the dramatic action which the poet desires.

Two very different images follow: the military picture of the town under siege, its commander made prisoner, and the betrothal image, culminating in the desire for the violence of sexual rape as the only adequate assault God can make in order to capture the poet's mind and spirit. It is typical of the poet who can use religious imagery in a poem of bitter love ('Twicknam Garden') that sexual imagery comes naturally into a divine poem. The restless, desperate energy of Donne's mind not only gives rise to such poetic imagery, but produces the self-tormenting vacillation of hope and despair which is the need he brings to God, for God to deal with.

Hymne to God my God, in my Sicknesse

Summary

1. As the poet approaches heaven, where he will join the choir of the saints and sing [praise] to God for ever, he prepares himself as man and as poet, considering at the threshold what he must do as he enters.

2. His doctors, with their devoted attention, are like geographers plotting the map of the poet's body. He can only lie flat on his bed while they show that this is his voyage of discovery to the south-west [the south represents the heat of fever, the west his decline], that through the straits of fever, he will pass to death.

3. The poet is joyful as he foresees his death, for although such a voyage can bring no return, how can death hurt him? If he is indeed a flat map, then east and west overlap, as do death and resurrection.

4. Is his permanent home in peaceful waters, or with the riches of the east, or even in Jerusalem, symbol of heavenly joy? Whichever way one journeys, it is through straits, the Anyan [possibly the Behring Straits], the Magellan or the Gibraltar; all the straits lead to distant parts of the world, Europe, Africa or Asia.

5. It is believed that the tree of knowledge in Paradise and the cross of Christ on Calvary were in the same place. God can see, as He looks at the poet, both Adams united in one person, the sweat [and pain] of the first Adam on his face, and, as he hopes, the blood of the second Adam [Christ] accepting his soul.

6. So in the purple cloak of Christ, the poet may be received by God, and through Christ's suffering and his own, he may attain the crown of glory. He has preached the word of God to others, and now chooses

as text for a sermon to himself the belief that Christ has brought him low in order to raise him high.

[For discussion of the theological ideas in this poem, see Chapter 3.]

Commentary

The 'Hymne to God my God' was probably written in 1623, when Donne was seriously ill and for a time not expected to recover. He charted the progress of his illness in a series of 'Devotions', and this poem has the same sense of approaching death combined with an analysis of his present position and his hope for God's mercy. It has also a sense of humour in adversity: the poet's eye sees the analogy of the doctors exploring his body to see what they can find and the map-makers trying to clarify the distant parts of the earth. He himself is no more or less than a flat map!

As so often, the thought of the poem is a logical progression from the everyday image of waiting on the doorstep, through the complexities of voyages of discovery and map-making, to mythology and a very immediate sense of his need to be accepted by God. The thought pattern is both complex and clear: complex mainly because of the weight of meaning put on single words or phrases, and clear because the path from one thought to another is precisely indicated.

The layers of meaning are often the result of 'double' images. The poet 'tunes the instrument' of his praise in heaven, that is, he prepares himself, but as he is also a poet, he tries to perfect his poetry so that it too will be found worthy. The pun on 'straits' as narrow passages of seaway and also extreme difficulties ('dire straits') is repeated. The distant parts of the world are suggested first by geographical and symbolic position (the Pacific Ocean, and the meaning of 'Pacific': peaceful) and then by reference to the old idea of the world being divided between the sons of Noah, Japheth receiving Europe, Ham getting Africa and Shem, Asia. Donne sees a coming together of Adam (the 'first Adam') and Christ (the 'second Adam') in the suffering which he himself is enduring, which is to him a crown of thorns. The single word 'purple' carries three layers of meaning: the poet's fever, the blood of Christ, and also the majesty of Christ. In the union of suffering and heavenly glory, the poet sees his hope: through the pain he can identify with Christ and therefore may be raised with Him.

Although there are difficult references and complex images in the poem, the most memorable ideas are probably, like the form of the verse, simple. Donne expresses his picture of heaven in a few short words: 'I shall be made thy musique', and his hope of everlasting life in a direct and moving line: 'So death doth touch the Resurrection'.

A Hymne to God the Father

Summary

1. Will God forgive the sin into which the poet was born, which became his own although it was committed before his lifetime? Will He also

forgive the sins which the poet deplores but seems unable to resist? Even if God does this. He has not finished [not gained Donne himself], for there are more.

2. Will God forgive the sin into which the poet has enticed others, leading them to sin? Will He forgive the sin which the poet managed to avoid for a short time, but was entrapped by for much longer? Even when God has done this, He has not finished [not gained Donne himself] for the poet has more.

3. The poet has a final sin of despair, that when his life ends, he will perish without reaching heaven. God must swear by His own Self that at the poet's death, Christ [the light-giving force] will shine on him as now and in the past. When God has done this, He will indeed have done [Donne]; there is no more fear.

Commentary

This famous poem, best known for the pun on the poet's name which forms its focal point and theme, is deceptively simple in appearance. There are no historical or astronomical images, no double layers of meaning. It is a seemingly simple prayer for God's mercy by the dying poet, probably written in 1623, under the same circumstances as the 'Hymne to God my God'. Yet the catalogue of sin is more than a simple list: it deepens in intensity. There is the original sin (see Chapter 3) into which the poet was born, his own sins, the sins into which he had led others, the sin which he has been unable over many years to escape, and finally the ultimate sin of despair.

The first and second verses are full of ideas and anxieties about sin, but the word is mentioned only once in the third verse, at the beginning. Donne faces this final, damning sin, and the emphasis on 'I' changes to an emphasis on 'thy'. The poet puts aside his own deep sense of unworthiness to look towards God and His Son (the 'sun', light of Donne's life), realising that in the light of divine mercy, even he will be accepted and therefore does not need to fear. So, of course, the sin of despair is avoided. Donne is clear-sighted enough to recognise, too, that however sinful his past life has been, he has known the light of Christ 'heretofore', as he does in this moment of writing. It is not a new faith which he is seeking, but a ratification of the God–man relationship which is already there.

The verse form is, of course, simple in that it is unusually regular, with the verse-long rhyme scheme, *ababab*, throwing the emphasis strongly on the short last line of each verse. The style is direct and conversational ('I' and 'my' occur very often). The poet is explaining to God the sins which torment him, and in so doing, he comes to the realisation of God's answer. Of course, the pun on his own name is the crux of each verse and the resolution of the last; it is typical of Donne to employ his wit even in an unusually strong affirmation of his faith.

4.2 GEORGE HERBERT

The Pearl

Summary
1. The poet is well acquainted with scholarship, both its sources and its output; he knows what reason has acquired from the observation of nature and also what it has produced for itself in laws and policy. He has learnt the secrets of astrology, what can easily be learnt from nature and what the scientist [alchemist] has to force from her. Discoveries of old and of recent date, learning inherited from the past and added to, causes and history: all these are either open to him or he has the keys by which to unlock them. Yet [above all] he loves God.

2. The poet is also acquainted with social preferment, and the profits gained from courtesy and wit, the contests for favours, whoever wins them, when ambition swells the heart and controls every expression of hand and eye. Such [glory] would tie the world in a love-knot to the poet's soul, and he must carry it as a burden wherever he goes. How much courage would it take to sell his life in this way either to friends or foes? Yet he loves God.

3. Pleasure, like music, is sweet, soothing and gives flavour to life. The passionate heart, the power of thought, laughter and music, whatever love and imagination have produced over two thousand years: all these are his. He knows about schemes to gain great wealth. He is made of flesh and blood, not metal, his senses are alive and often complain that they have a greater part of his being than what controls them, who is but one against five. Yet his love is for God.

4. All these things he knows and has at his disposal. Therefore it is not in blind ignorance, but with eyes open that he flies to God, fully understanding the bargain struck and the benefits involved, the rate and cost of God's love, and all the conditions that apply. Yet through all the complexities of life, it is not the poet's own humble intelligence but the silk cord which God lets down from heaven to him and guides and teaches him how by it to climb to God Himself.

Commentary
George Herbert often gave his poems titles which are biblical references containing the theme of the whole poem. In this case, he gives the reference, Matthew XIII, 45, although it is clearer if we quote both verses 45 and 46, from the Authorised Version which Herbert must have known and used at Bemerton:

> Again, the kingdom of heaven is like unto a merchant man, seeking goodly pearls: Who, when he had found one pearl of great price, went and sold all that he had, and bought it.

'The pearl' of the title is God's grace and the poet's response (for a definition of 'grace', see Chapter 3); the poem describes the 'all that he had' which was to be sold in order that the pearl should be acquired. Herbert is not despising wordly success and pleasure; like Marvell after him, he enjoys and appreciates beauty, especially the beauty of music. Nevertheless, such things must not distract man from the most important need of his life, the 'pearl'.

At first sight, the poem may appear to be boastful, the poet claiming so much achievement for himself. It is probably more true to say that he would have rejected false modesty. He was a scholar, and as Public Orator at Cambridge, he had a scholar's achievement and hope for a brilliant future reasonably before him. Indeed, his analysis in the first verse of the different ways in which knowledge is gained (by reason, observation of nature, on the foundations of the past, by new discoveries both mental and geographical) shows the order and insight of his mind. The layers of meaning, too, show a complexity of thought. The wine press from which the wine runs is presumably teaching, especially the teaching of the university; the overtones of the printing press at the same time suggest wide reading as another natural source of learning.

Herbert was born into a wealthy family closely related to the Earls of Pembroke, and by his mother's second marriage he gained a stepfather of title and influence. A brilliant career at Court seemed natural for one whose birth and talents so combined; he did indeed know about ambition for preferment, and was also aware that it could be a trap, the selling of his soul either to those who supported him or those who opposed him. He obviously had wit, spirit and a love of music. All that he describes was indeed at his disposal. So Herbert clearly understands the bargain he has to make (he is very fond of images from business and commerce); he knows what he must be ready, if necessary, to forgo. He makes his theological position clear (see Chapter 3) by recognising that in the end, his own strengths and achievements are not sufficient to bring him to salvation. It is the combination of the grace of God and his own response (the climb) which will give him the pearl of great price.

The character of Herbert comes through the poem strongly: he is a man of ability, position, ambition, who has to work out for himself the priorities of his life, and he has done so. Interestingly, in this poem as usually in Herbert's poetry, the effort is in the past ('*did* both conduct and teach me. . .'). While Donne fights his battles through his poetry, so that the reader works through them alongside the poet, Herbert's gentler struggles are seen with hindsight, so that the reader sees how it *was*, rather than how it *is*. Nevertheless, this does not prevent a sense of strong personal feeling in the poem.

The verses are long (10 lines), bound together partly by the rhyme scheme, *ababccdede*, and partly by the constant use of the first person (I, my). Often, the lines have a heavy break in the middle (comma or semicolon), and a quarter of the lines run on: the combination of these two techniques gives a sense of movement and variety to the verse.

Herbert's imagery is wide, although the reference to 'new-found seas' is much rarer in his work than in Donne's. Much more typical of Herbert are the immediate, everyday images of the housewife spinning, the true-love-knot, and (a favourite of his) the silk cord. The commercial imagery, the stock and surplus, the main sale and the commodities, the rate and price, is also often intermingled with the homely images, as if work and home were the important constituents of one part of his life, the other being the Church. The drama, such as it is, is quiet and gentle. The problem is posed, with the repeated final line 'Yet I love thee', and resolved, as so often in Herbert's poetry, in the final line of the last verse, 'climbe to thee'.

Redemption

Summary
The 'I' of the story told in this poem has been for a long time the tenant of a wealthy landlord. His affairs have not prospered, and so at last he plucks up courage to go to ask his lord to cancel the current lease and to make a new one which will demand a lower rent.

Going to heaven, to his lord's manor, he is told that the lord has recently gone away on business, to take possession of some land which he had bought at great cost, long ago.

The man returns at once, and, considering the high rank of his lord, he looks for him in the great resorts, cities, theatres, gardens, parks and courts. Eventually, he hears the sound of a crowd of poor people, and the laughter of thieves and murderers. There, he sees his lord, who immediately grants the man's suit, and dies.

Commentary
It is unusual for a sonnet to tell a story, but Herbert manages to compress an introduction, action and resolution into his fourteen lines with the apparent simplicity born of great skill. He is always adept at writing concisely, choosing his words with precision and knowing exactly when to stop (a quality not always shared by his admirer, Henry Vaughan). The close resemblance of 'Redemption' to a biblical parable has been seen before (notably in the excellent *An Introduction to the Metaphysical Poets* by Patricia Beer), and in the simple language, clear storyline and familiar imagery, it is indeed a dramatic parable in its own right.

'Redemption' is dramatic in a different way from, for example, Donne's 'Holy Sonnet xiv', also in its way about redemption. Herbert also uses a conversational, colloquial start ('Having been tenant. . .'), but as usual his conversation is a quiet, gentle one, in this case, the telling of a story. Nevertheless, the relationship between the characters is clear, and would be familiar to Herbert's readers. The rich lord, often absent on business, or by choice, would be expected to frequent theatres and parks, as did the nobility in seventeenth-century London. The tenant is dependent on the generosity of his lord for his own well-being and indeed livelihood. (Vivid pictures of the great estate and its owner's responsibilities towards tenants and servants are drawn in poetry by Ben Jonson, in 'Penshurst', and by Thomas Carew, in 'To Saxham'.) The lord can either accept the tenant's suit or reject it out of hand, and the tenant (probably, in Jacobean England, not very literate, remote from the life of cities and lawyers) is threatened with the failure of his crops or animals and has to throw himself on his lord's mercy. It is a vivid picture of the life of the time, and many of Herbert's readers must have nodded in agreement: this is how it is.

The drama of the poem lies also in the sudden change to direct speech at the end. There has been conversation previously, but it has been the voice of the storyteller, and by report the voices of the lord's servants at his manor. Suddenly, and without introduction, four words spoken by the apparently rather remote landlord are directed to the storyteller and to the reader, and the device produces an immediacy startling in its effect. Nevertheless, the story itself is a foregone conclusion. The reader knows, as soon as the nature of the parable becomes clear, not only where the lord will be found, but what his response will be; they also know his fate. In that sense, the poem is undramatic, except that, as Patricia Beer has pointed out, there is a sense in which great literature can always have the same effect: we can be apprehensive, afraid, made tense, surprised, again and again, no matter how well we know the outcome, and this is true of Herbert's sonnet.

The sonnet form is controlled by the needs of the story; as a result there are two 'background' sections, which form the octet, (*abab*, *cdcd*), the 'turn' at the start of the sestet to the subsequent action (*effe*) and the resolution in the final couplet (*gg*). The lines are varied, as in 'The Pearl', by internal division and enjambment (running-on). The movement is rapid partly because of the telling of the story and partly because of the compression of language. 'Ragged noise' suggests in two words all the bustle and poverty of the Jacobean city.

Herbert was both poet and priest, and saw himself as a teacher, guiding and helping not only his parishioners but also his fellow priests. As in the morality plays which 'Redemption' resembles, the story may be well-known, but it is given new life and emphasis in the telling. Herbert draws from a little picture of contemporary life the story of man's redemption and God's grace. As in 'The Pearl', it is the grace of God which is paramount: the tenant is granted his suit before he has even asked.

Easter Wings

Summary

1. [The poet speaks to God.] Man was created by God with wealth and abundance, but through foolishness he lost Paradise [see Chapter 3], and so declined increasingly until he became very poor. The poet asks to rise with Christ, singing harmoniously as larks do of Christ's vic-

tories. Then the effect of the Fall will be to make the resurrection of the poet more intense.

2. When he was young, the poet knew sorrow, and his sins resulted in sickness and shame, so that he became wasted away. He prays to be united with Christ, and to share His Easter victory, for if he is grafted onto the strength of Christ, affliction will merely make his resurrection greater.

Commentary

The immediate impact of 'Easter Wings' is visual: the poem has the physical shape of wings. Some readers today may feel that such a device is artificial and over-clever, but it was less strange to a seventeenth-century reader, and Herbert himself used it frequently. He was a master of such metrical ingenuity, devising 116 different verse forms, none of them repeated. Perhaps his deep love of music influenced the metre, encouraging him to combine sense with sound not just in single words or lines, but through a whole poem. Certainly the movement and sound of 'Easter Wings' symbolise the flight of the lark and also its song.

The skill of the poem is shown not just in its metrical pattern and by the echoing of the lark's movement in the story of the Fall and redemption of man, but in such a wealth of technique producing a poem of such ecstasy. The depth of the poet's faith and his joy at Easter are evident and the sense of victory is personal and strong. D. J. Enright accurately said of Herbert that he has 'one of the strongest poetic personalities in English'. This personality is seen more forcefully in greater poems, such as 'The Collar', but it is not lacking here in this ingenious poem.

The decline in man's state after the Fall is shown as the lines also become 'most poor', shorter and less emphatic. At the seventh line, after the stressed 'With thee', the lines grow again, rising to the word 'victories', followed by the long comment line, showing the relationship between the Fall and the Resurrection and also in effect between Good Friday and Easter. The pattern is repeated in the second verse. Sorrow, sickness and shame have attended the poet. (It is a little difficult to associate 'shame' with Herbert, but he probably thinks of the worldly ambition which tempted him in his youth.) He, and the verse, become 'most thinne'. After the repeated stress of 'With thee' (it is Christ Who brings about the change), the lines rise again to 'victorie', and the final two lines again comment on Christ's suffering and Resurrection. The only image in the poem, apart from the lark, is from falconry: a falcon's damaged wing could be strengthened by 'imping', grafting in new feathers. The bird/wing image is in keeping with the poem as a whole.

The lark, noted for the height at which it hovers and the beauty of its song, is a superb symbol of resurrection, and the rise and fall of its flight and its singing are suggested vividly by the movement of the poem; the title unites both theme and symbol with remarkable economy.

62

The Collar

Summary

ll. 1–8   The poet angrily strikes the table, declaring that he can take no
more, but will go abroad. Why should he always be sighing and
pining away? His future and his life are free [from restraint], as
free as the road, formless as the wind, as liberal as a harvest
store. Why should he still be begging like a suitor at Court? Is all
the harvest he can produce a thorn, making him bleed, without
any fruit to restore his heart in compensation?

ll. 9–16   Once there was wine, before it was dried up by his sighs. There
was corn before it was washed away by his tears. Is he the only
one whose year is totally lost? Has he no crown of laurels [the
crown of a poet] to demonstrate his success? Are there no
flowers or garlands, but are all blasted and wasted?

II. 17–26   It is not so. There is a harvest and he has hands to take it. He can
recover all the years lost to sighing by enjoying himself to the
full. He must leave the lifeless dispute of what is or is not fitting,
get out of the cage which imprisons him, and which is no more
than a rope of sand, made of trivial thoughts. It has seemed to
him like a stout rope to force him, to drag him along like an
imprisoning law. All the time his eyes have been closed so that
he could not see the truth.

ll. 27–32   He will go abroad, and his captor must take heed. Reminders of
death should be put away, the poet's own fears must be tied up.
Anyone who refuses to follow and serve his own need deserves
the burden he carries.

ll. 33–36   But even as the poet raves and becomes more fierce and wild,
he hears a voice calling him 'Child' and he replies 'My Lord'.

Commentary

This is the most famous and the most dramatic of Herbert's poems. It
begins with something of the urgency of Donne's poetic beginnings:
personal, active, fierce. The poet feels restricted, hemmed in by the
demands of his faith: the collar of the title suggests both a controlling
force and also a needed restraint; it has overtones also of *choler*, the anger
and heightened emotion which the poet feels. Herbert's struggles are never
about the existence of God or the rightness of the Christian faith. They are
about his own relationship with God, and so this poem divides into three,
two aspects of the poet's feelings (yearning for freedom, determination to
be free) followed by a direct conversation with God.

The restless turning this way and that which is the subject of the greater
part of the poem is echoed in the verse form. It too is free from inner
restraint, escaping all set patterns, but it is not without form. Herbert is
far too great a poet to allow his poem to become weak or uncontrolled.

The verse is sinewy, strong, full of positive statements, questions, imagery which weaves to and fro with the poet's emotions. The long line/short line suggests (as often in Herbert's poetry) struggle followed by resolution, but in 'The Collar' there is also a sense of rising panic, as the short lines crowd one another with interwoven rhymes, before the final quatrain. The rhymes are, in fact, a clear indication of the form of the poem. Since rhyme represents a unifying, regulating force, it is uneven and erratic at first (*more* in l. 1 waits for *store* in l. 5; *thorn* in l. 7 for *corn* in l. 11, and, most extreme, *pine* in l. 3 for *wine* in l. 10). As the poem gathers speed and urgency, the rhymes start to gather, not always as full rhymes, sometimes as echoes (*draw/law*, *heed/need*, *fears/forbears*, *abroad/load*; *abroad*, of course, picks up the vowel sound of *draw/law*). Then with the dramatic resolution, the rhyme suddenly becomes peacefully regular, *abab*, as the conflict is over.

The final quatrain is a typical *volte face* by Herbert. He has built up his poem with perfect control to a near-hysterical demand for freedom, and then suddenly turns his argument upside-down. In the middle of his raving about freedom from restraint, he hears God calling him as a father calls a child, out of love, not compulsion. In his reply, the poet acknowledges the call as that of a Father Who is also his Lord. The rope is of sand not because the poet can by his own efforts break it but because it is formed of a loving relationship.

The pattern of words has an intellectual complexity which is also reminiscent of Donne's writing. In the first twelve lines, for instance, there is an interweaving of the layers of meaning: they overlap and integrate in another echo of the poet's restless mood. So the pattern: *board-store-harvest-fruit-corn*, leads from the table which is symbolically struck to the bread of the Mass; the pattern; *board-thorn-blood-cordiall-wine*, leads from the table to the wine of the Mass. (The thorn reminds the reader of the Crown of Thorns; cordiall means 'of the heart', with overtones of heart's blood.) These lines seem to be trying to escape from the altar and the Mass, and yet fail to do so, as the poet is trying to break free from the constraints of his faith.

At the same time, the words are homely and familiar, words which are full of significance in everyday life. As H. Coombes points out in *Literature and Criticism* (Pelican, 1953), Herbert uses things which are physical, which can be handled, tasted, which hurt the body (like the thorn) or cheer it: 'the words themselves have the solidity and firmness that make us call them 'real'.' The poet is experiencing his struggle partly because he is so closely involved with ordinary life; from the harvest to the 'good cable', he sees the spiritual battlefield as the life of the priest and his parish, his own struggle is that of other 'ordinary' Christians. The emotions he feels are anger, frustration, even self-pity (is it only me?), a refusal to be confined, an apparently carefree bravado, followed by a deeper understanding of the nature of his relationship with God. Herbert understands himself and in the poem analyses his own varying moods; he does so with sensitivity and enormous technical skill. The result is for him an unusual force

64

and passion, and a poem which tells the reader much about human desires, fullness of life, the relationship of God and man, and about George Herbert himself.

Love

Summary

1. Love bids the guest welcome, but he draws back, feeling unworthy because unclean and sinful. Love is quick to notice the hesitation after his guest's entry, and comes to him to ask if he needs anything.

2. The guest declares his own unworthiness, but Love calls him a worthy guest. This meets with protest: the guest is unkind, ungrateful, and, much as he loves his host, he cannot even raise his eyes to him. Love takes his guest by the hand, and smilingly asks who made the eyes if he himself did not.

3. The truth of this is acknowledged, but the guest has damaged his host's creation. He is full of shame, and would go only where he is a deserving guest. Love gently points out that any blame has already been borne. In a last attempt, the guest asks to be allowed to serve at table. Love insists instead that he sit and partake of the feast. The guest can resist no longer, and sits to eat.

Commentary

It is almost impossible to summarise this beautiful poem in straight prose. Like 'Redemption', it is a small story, a dramatic parable, made up of a conversation between two close and loving friends.

The story tells one short incident, developed gently and resolved in great simplicity of language. Nevertheless, it presents a vivid picture. The guest feels dusty, not fit to sit at the table of his friend. Love is 'quick-eyed' (a typical Herbert personification, hardly felt as such because Love is already established as a character). With the tact and courtesy of the good host, he asks 'if I lack'd anything'. The conversation develops, with the guest torn between the need to stress his unworthiness and his obvious affection for his host (he uses the loving, familiar 'my deare'). Love also presses his claim, but with warmth (taking the hand of his guest), a smile, and the gentlest of puns on 'eye' and 'I'. The exchange continues into the last verse, with the guest emphasising that he has no rightful place and Love removing all objections. The 'blame' for man's sin and unworthiness has already been borne by Christ on the cross. Finally the guest offers to serve, Love insists on his taking his place, and the conversation ends with six short, one-syllable words, in the order of normal prose: 'So I did sit and eat.'

It is a turnabout like that of 'The Collar', but lacking in tension (the character of the host is clear from the start) and with a quiet, regular rhythm and rhyme scheme which emphasises the atmosphere of two friends talking: there is no real argument. The long/short line lengths again suggest conflict and resolution, but the conflict is simply the hesitation to accept the grace of God (typically, it is God Who takes the lead, and the poet has only to respond, as in 'The Pearl'), followed by the final acceptance.

A poem of such simplicity and such deep emotion could easily have been sentimental. Herbert avoids this by the parable-like form, the attention to detail which makes the scene vivid, and the understatement. Diction, rhythm and rhyme are tightly controlled. The result is a perfect poem, deeply moving in its simplicity and as an expression of the joy and acceptance of the poet's own faith.

4.3 HENRY VAUGHAN

The Retreate

Summary

ll. 1–20   The poet was happy in his childhood, when he still had the brightness of an angel about him. That was before he understood the nature of the place in which the second part of his existence was to be lived, and his soul had not yet learnt to imagine anything but pure, heavenly thoughts. He had not then walked more than a mile or two from the love he knew first [Christ], and looking back over so short a distance, could catch a glimpse of the brightness of His face. Sometimes, gazing for an hour at a golden cloud or a flower, he could see in such lesser beauty some weak shadow of what eternity might be.

At such time, the poet had not yet taught his tongue to speak sinfully, wounding his conscience, nor had he the evil art to provide a separate sin for each of his senses. Instead, he was aware through his whole being of the bright blossoming of eternal life.

ll. 21–26   Now, the poet longs to travel back, to retrace that earlier journey. So might he once more reach the plain where he first lost his early brightness, from which place a pure spirit might see the city shaded by palm trees [Jericho].

ll. 27–32   But alas, the poet's soul has stayed too long in earthly life, and is drunk, staggering on its way. Some men love to move forward, but he would choose to go backwards, so that when his body turns to dust which is placed in his funerary urn, he himself would be back in the state of being in which he had set out.

Commentary

'The Retreate' is a perfectly balanced, controlled poem, concise in a way not always achieved by Vaughan, and revealing many aspects of thought which are typical of his writing. Human existence is seen as being in three parts: the before-birth stage in heaven, angelic in quality and marked by a close communion with Christ; human life on earth, marked by an increasing distance from Christ, and damaged by sin; life after death, eternal life, sharing through grace the heavenly state of the first stage. William Wordsworth's ode: 'Intimations of Immortality' has often been noted as similar: both poets see childhood as not far removed from the glories of life before birth, but the glory slowly fades in all the complexities and evils of the world.

The poem divides into two parts. The poet first looks back at his early life, using for it many of the words often associated with the symbolism of his writing: *shine*, *white* (symbol of innocence and purity), *bright* (repeated). Typical also of Vaughan is the relationship of nature to faith. Nature is the creation of God and reveals God in beauty, light and praise, for nature is not damaged by the worldliness of man. So the cloud, golden perhaps at sunrise or sunset, and the flower are to Vaughan 'weaker glories' which echo the glories of heaven. Man learns from nature to look towards God and to enjoy the beauty around him. Henry Vaughan's twin brother Thomas was a famous Hermetic philosopher, and Henry translated some Hermetic writings from Latin. The ideas, taught by this philosophy, that the soul is formed of the union of light and life, and that nothing is destructible, influenced the poet, and probably help to explain the stress on eternal life and the number of 'light' images in his work.

Vaughan was also something of a mystic, and in this he is very different from his great poetic influence, George Herbert, and from Wordsworth. At times, Vaughan's whole poem is made radiant by a single line which it is difficult to explain fully in literal prose. The reader may or may not *understand* the line, but beyond intellectual understanding there is a spiritual illumination which comes of suggestion and overtone rather than precise definition. In the best of his work, such lines can move the reader beyond the power of thought, and in 'The Retreate' there is a particularly beautiful example, striking in its natural image of the 'buds' of eternity which the child still holds, and superb in its total effect: 'Bright shootes of everlastingnesse.'

The second part of the poem records the second stage of the poet's existence. It is possible for man to glimpse 'Jericho' (biblical home of God's elect), but his soul is too drunk to know where it is going. The sudden transition to a down-to-earth, very human image echoes the change from the 'shadows of eternity' state to that of humanity out of control, lacking in vision, simply drunk. Vaughan takes up the idea of the inebriated man staggering backwards and forwards, to end his poem with a metaphysical paradox worthy of Donne. He wants to go backwards on his forward journey through life in order to arrive at the state in which he started. The language is now realistic (*dust, urn*) and emphatic: the break in the normally regular rhythm which occurs in the last line gives great stress to 'in that state' and a heavy emphasis to the whole line, linking it in thought to the beginning of the poem. Vaughan does not often compress so much meaning, imagery and quiet drama into so short a piece. In spite of the couplet form, the rhymes are not intrusive, perhaps because the lines so often run on, and the rhythmical pattern has enough slight variation to bring it closer to ordinary speech (one of Herbert's gifts to his follower) while still preserving the movement and flow of the whole.

The Morning-Watch

Summary

ll. 1–9 The poet awakens with a sense of joy and infinite felicity; his soul like budding flowers bursts into life. Through the long night, sleep enfolded him in curtains like a shroud and the clouds of darkness the dew of the Holy Spirit fell on him, and now it gives him new life and energy.

ll. 9–22 As he listens, he hears the whole created world singing praise as it moves; the winds, waterfalls, birds, animals, all things adore God in their own ways. So the universe is whirled round in God-ordained praise and order, the harmonious sound of nature itself. Prayer is the music of the world in harmony with God, the spirit of man and the sound of his praise echoing to the joy of the listening heaven.

ll. 22–33 So the poet asks to reach God when he lies down to sleep. The devout soul at night is like starlight through clouds, shedding some light towards the earth, but above the clouds shining and moving beyond the misty cloud-cover. So whether he is asleep in his curtained bed or turned to ashes in his grave, the poet's soul will still abide in God.

Commentary

The title of this poem suggests a religious vigil, and Vaughan is indeed writing of the awakening of the soul to an ecstasy of prayer and praise, echoed in a universal hymn of joy and adoration. Everything which God created joins in this hymn: the animals, the natural world, man himself and the stars and planets. There is no disharmony in the poet's vision of universal praise.

The lyrical, singing quality of 'The Morning-Watch' is typical of much of Vaughan's writing, as is the mysticism which produces a wonderful *sense* of joy without clearly defined intellectual concepts. 'The great chime and symphony of nature' is difficult to analyse, and yet its intention and significance are clear, especially when 'symphony' is thought of in its basic meaning of harmony, agreement. The music imagery, most of all the key image 'Prayer is the world in tune', is reflected in the music of the poem, the sweeping emotional force which carries the reader with it. Vaughan achieves this partly by his choice of words and partly by the rhythm/rhyme patterns.

Many of the words reflect Vaughan's vision: *joys, infinite sweetness, adore, bliss*. The awakening is linked at once to nature in the flower imagery (*shoots, buds*) and the union of the spirit of man and the created universe in their common act of worship weaves through the poem. Prayer is an essentially human activity, but it is the whole world which is in tune. Vaughan's ecstasy takes him beyond the limits of human time and place, even though at the end the poem comes firmly back to his own life and death. The waking and sleeping of a human being (the paradox of 'let me climbe when I lye down' is part of this) is united with the rise and fall of nature, the endless seasons, the boundless motion of the turning world. So the movement is caught by the words (*rest*, *fell*, *quick* (meaning living), *awakes*, *rising*, *falling*, the echo to heaven, *climbe*, *lye down*, the star above the clouds, the *curtain'd grave*) and also by the rhythm. The ecstatic start, the quiet sounds of *rest*, *still*, *clouds*, contrast with the energy of *Blouds and Spirits*, *awakes and sings*; the tempo increases to the near-violence of *hurl'd* and is then slowed by the longer lines and gentler tone. There is another, less marked, gain in speed at the short lines which run-on from *though said* to *are above*, and the two last lines with their interwoven ideas of sleep and death are slow, with long vowel sounds (*grave*, *sleep*) and commas adding pauses to the line length.

The strange rhyme scheme helps with this rise and fall of the poem. At times, the rhymes are close together (*sings*, *springs*, *things*) and emphasised by echoes which are not true rhymes (*sings*, *winds*; *chime*, *tune*), but the poet also interweaves rhymes at distance from one another (*buds*, *Blouds*; *said*, *bed*). The resolution of the poem within the life and death of the poet himself is shown by the only two long lines which rhyme, the final couplet. Such a feeling of firm faith reflected in close rhyme at the end of a poem may well be part of Vaughan's inheritance from Herbert (see the rhyme scheme of 'The Collar').

The range of images in the poem is wide, although very different from that of Donne, and in many ways from that of Herbert. The nature imagery, the budding flower, the clouded star, is more typical of Vaughan than of any other Metaphysical poet, and the sense of light and mist (often the mist over water) comes to him directly from the Welsh scenery of his beloved Brecon Beacons. Music has already been mentioned as a frequent source of imagery. Less striking, perhaps, is the awareness of the blood containing the vital spirits which give life, but the association of blood with 'circulation' reminds us abruptly that this visionary poet was also a practical country doctor, well aware of the circulation of the blood. Images of sleep and death are interwoven throughout the poem, from the 'still shrouds of sleep' to the 'curtained grave'. The final couplet is full of references to both: the bed is but a grave with curtains, sleep is like ashes, hiding both the lamp (at the bedside) and the poet's life. There is a feeling of security in the poet's faith as he is able to see death as merely a going to sleep in God's hands.

The reader must be intrigued by the visual pattern of the poem. Unlike Herbert, Vaughan did not normally produce pictures such as that of 'Easter Wings', but he did follow the older poet's long line/short line representation of struggle and resolution: in this poem, it is the long lines which carry the resolution. However, there is a pattern in that the sections represented by long and short lines number nine, which is a mystical number (nine orders of angels, nine planetary spheres, etc.). Such a patterning seems strange to a modern reader, but it is in keeping with Vaughan's visionary turn of mind and his sense of unity – the unity of man with nature and of both with God, the unity of the three stages of man's existence, before-birth, earthly life and after-death, and the unity of these three stages through man's abiding with God in eternity.

The World

Summary

1. The poet had a vision of eternity, a ring [symbol of eternity] of pure, unending light. It was peaceful and bright, and below it time, divided by the movement of the spheres, moved like a vast shadow. Within the shadow, the world and its stars were in celestial motion.

   On earth, the poet saw the [typical] doting lover, with fantastical melody, singing mournfully; beside him were his lute, his imagination, his dreams, bitter humour as well as gloves and love-knots, the trivialities of pleasure. Yet his true treasure was scattered around, while he wept over a flower.

2. The shadowy figure of the statesman, weighed down with problems and woes, like a thick fog at midnight moved so slowly that he could not be seen either to come or go. Damning thoughts, like dismal eclipses of the sun, scowl at his soul, and witnesses [against him] cry in crowds, pursuing him. This devious politician digs deep and works underground in order not to be seen, and there he clutches his prey. Yet God sees his cunning, though he battens on holy things, considers perjury like insignificant insects, and produces around him bloodshed and weeping, of which he takes little notice.

3. The miser sits, terrified, on his heap of earthly treasure, pining away his life, hardly trusting himself with his precious dust. He will not place one piece of his treasure in heaven, but lives in constant fear of thieves. There are thousands like him, hugging their own skins about themselves. On the other hand, the downright epicure places his heaven in the gratification of his senses, scorning to pretend otherwise, while others, almost as bad, slip gradually into great excess. Weaker men, enslaved by slight, trivial possessions, think themselves fine, while poor, despised truth sits by, counting the victories of temptation.

4. Yet there were some who, all this time, between singing [praise] and weeping [for sin] soared up into the ring [of eternity]. Most would not take wing, and the poet sees them as fools to prefer dark night to the light of truth, to live in grottoes and caves and hate daylight because it shows them the way to escape from the darkness and deadness of the world to God. By choosing that way, they might reach the brightness of the sun, and even exceed it.

But even as the poet so discusses their foolishness, he hears a whisper which says that this ring is provided by the Bridegroom only for His bride [that is, by Christ for those who. come to Him willingly].

[Vaughan finishes with a quotation from the first epistle of St John, (II, 16 and 170 which shows the inspiration and the theme of the poem.]

Commentary

In spite of his mysticism, Vaughan was a practical man (trained as a lawyer, practising as a doctor) with a great affection for his fellow man, as is clear from this poem. He grieves for the sinful world and its refusal to accept the offered grace of God, but when he looks at human beings, it is with a gentle laughter at their foibles rather than with bitterness or distaste. The sense of humour which this poem reveals, its realism and its affection, make it most attractive to the modern reader.

The first two lines, probably the most often quoted in all Vaughan's writing, are visionary as his work so often is, and the use of phrases like 'pure and endless light' is reminiscent of the 'white celestiall thought' of 'The Retreate'; the radiance and sense of transcendent joy is like that of 'The Morning-Watch'. Nevertheless, Vaughan was, like many of his contemporaries, haunted by time and the conflict of time and eternity in which human beings live. So within his great vision of eternity, there is the world, and within the world human beings wasting their time in a variety of ways, as human beings do. The miniatures which Vaughan paints of some of his characters are vivid and dramatic, and appealing to readers of all time. They may be caricatures, but in a few precise words the poet brings them to individual life, so that we also laugh at them, but ruefully and perhaps shamefacedly. The lover is behaving as foolishly as those in love do, weeping over a favour from his beloved, losing all sense of proportion and ignoring the more solemn aspects of life.

Vaughan's drawing of the statesman, influenced by the English idea of Niccolò Machiavelli, is perhaps the mot powerful of all; it may well have been written soon after the Civil War, and gives a dramatic insight into the mentality of those who seek for power with ruthlessness combined with the instinct for self-preservation. Weighed down by his office, such a man lives in a fog which makes any clear moral decision difficult; inwardly he is aware of the evil he does, and outwardly he is hounded by his victims. Yet he is devious, working through others, secretly, in order to catch his enemies unaware. He is without scruple or mercy, and only God clearly sees his action.

The miser is a more light-hearted caricature, delightfully afraid even to trust his own hands with his treasure, and hugging himself to himself in a life of constant fear. Those who live for sensual pleasure are of different sorts, some open and wholehearted, some falling bit by bit into excess, some merely ensnared by materialism: truth (true worth) is despised by them all. Some human beings, however, have a genuine awareness of sin and a heart full of praise, and for them, eternity awaits. Vaughan's picture of the faithful lacks the attractive detail which brings his sinners to life, but the poem ends with his acceptance that if man has free will, he will use it for evil as well as for good. The last two lines are ambiguous in that they could be read as a justification of predestination, widely accepted at the time (see Chapter 3). However, in the light of Vaughan's royalist, high-Church position, it is very unlikely that he would have interpreted the text in that way.

The imagery of 'The World' includes the visionary (the ring of the second line, or the vast shadow in 1. 6) and the natural (the midnight-fog, the gnats and flies), but above all it is biblical, both in wide application and in detail. So the miser is drawn directly from the Gospel of St Matthew, (VI, 19):

> Lay not up for yourselves treasures upon earth, where moth and rust doth corrupt, and where thieves break through and steal. . .

while the 'clouds of crying witnesses' is an echo, conscious or otherwise, of the Epistle to the Hebrews, (XII, 1), 'encompassed about with so great a cloud of witnesses. . .'. Vaughan was not, as were his predecessors Donne and Herbert, an ordained priest, but he was widely read in theology and had a love of the Bible which made its words come readily to his mind.

The rhyme scheme of the poem is unusual in having three rhyming lines at the start of each verse, before the couplets; the rhythm is varied by the long/short lines and the frequent run-on lines; as so often, the poem follows the voice rhythms as Herbert's does, with a gentle ironical emphasis from time to time (as on *flower* at the end of the first verse).

Like the previous poems by Vaughan, 'The World' has a sense of unity; the poet can see a vision of eternity, radiant and joyful, without for a moment losing sight of the complexities of ordinary life: his 'good' souls see the pure and endless light and fly to it, while his 'mole' not only digs below the ground but is himself, of course, blind.

Man

Summary
1. The poet considers the steadfastness and stability of some insignificant creatures which live on earth, where birds tell the silent passage of time like alert clocks, and where bees at night go home to their hives and flowers open early with the sun and close as the sun sets.

2. He wishes that God would give the constancy of these things to man. They keep always to God's divine ordinances and allow no business to interrupt their peaceful existence. The birds do not sow or reap, and yet they eat and drink, the flowers have no clothes, and yet Solomon was never clad so richly.

3. Man is always concerned with trifles or cares. He has no roots and does not stay still in one place, but in a restless and erratic fashion moves about the earth. He knows he belongs somewhere, but can

hardly remember the place; he says it is so far away that he has forgotten how to return.

4. So he knocks at everyone's door, strays and roams around, lacking even the sense of a [magnetic] loadstone to draw him home in the darkest night, inspired by some hidden sense given by God. Man is like a shuttle, weaving in and out through the looms, in whose destiny God ordered movement but granted no rest.

Commentary

The influence of George Herbert is seen most strongly in this poem. The theme, man's constant searching which contrasts with the reliability of nature, but which is God-ordained in the very creation of human beings, is reminiscent of Herbert's 'The Pulley', in which God gives man 'repining restlessnesse'. The simple, direct language is also like Herbert's, especially the conversational 'I would (said I). . .'.

Yet there are aspects of the poem which are typical of Vaughan. The sensitivity to nature and the delightful natural imagery ('birds like watchful clocks') is very much Vaughan's style, as is the direct biblical quotation of the second verse (the Gospel of St Matthew, (VI, 26 and 28-9):

Behold the fowls of the air: for they sow not, neither do they reap, nor gather into barns; yet your heavenly Father feedeth them. . . . . .Consider the lilies of the field, how they grow; they toil not, neither do they spin: And yet I say unto you, that even Solomon in all his glory was not arrayed like one of these.

The most vivid image, however, is the simplest and most familiar: 'Man is the shuttle', which surprises the reader and yet is most satisfying because of its immediacy and its originality. Simplicity of diction, too, is striking. The language has a strong feeling of quiet conversation, even to the monosyllabic, almost childlike quality of:

He sayes it is so far
That he hath quite forgot how to go there.

If it is childlike, this is intentional, for Vaughan's picture of man is of a being running around without much sense of direction, becoming confused and helpless, endlessly asking questions, yet always precious to the poet and to his Maker.

Quickness

Summary

1. False life is a deception and nothing more; when will it disappear, and stop deceiving men by preventing their seeing true life?

2. Such a false life is a useless enterprise, a blind, self-imposed state of being, like the storm of waves and wind debating their power.

3. True life is a constant, discerning light, a joy aware of its own source, not accidental or temporary, but always bright, calm, full, never cloying.

4. It is so joyful that it constantly gives vitality, shining, happy, pleasing even outside eternity.

5. A false existence is a deep-digging mole, or, less than that, a moving mist. Its opposite is inexpressible: a quality of life irradiated by the love of God.

Commentary

Dr Johnson commented of Vaughan that 'he trembles upon the brink of meaning', and this is nowhere more true than of 'Quickness'. It is difficult to define the title: something like 'a vital quality of life' ('quick' in its old meaning of 'alive'), but more than that, and so it is with the poem as a whole. Its theme and outline are clear: the poet is contrasting the emptiness of a false life, without God, with the joyful life spent in acceptance of God's love. Yet the details are not clear, and constantly evade intellectual analysis. The strength of the poem – and it is majestically and movingly strong – lies in its power of suggestion. We do not necessarily know what Vaughan means; we have to respond.

Some aspects can be analysed. False life is a foil, like the backcloth used by a jeweller to set off a precious stone, or perhaps also a defeat (we are *foiled* of true life). It is also moonlike. The moon pulls the tides to and fro with an enormous force, and yet the movement seems pointless and the exertion of force wasted. In a storm at sea, the wind and the waves seem to be struggling with one another, and yet neither will win. Later in the poem, Vaughan describes false life again as a mole, digging around in the dark of the earth, or as mere inanimate mist, moving to confuse human beings. As Patricia Beer has pointed out, Vaughan lived in the country for almost all of his life, and he has a love of the play of mist and light. Moles and mists were not unattractive to him, in spite of the obvious dangers of sudden mist on a mountainous landscape. False life is not easily put aside; it has its attractions.

The true life which is Vaughan's contrast is also analysed. It is constant, a light which not only does not move but which is 'discerning'; it understands its own source and quality. It can never become cloying, but always 'vivifies', which is much more than its dictionary definition of 'enliven, animate'. Even within the limits of human existence, it is able to give satisfaction and joy. But the final effect of Vaughan's poem cannot be so analysed. The style is simple, the language not complex. It is the power of suggestion which matters, the build-up of words (*light, joy, bright, calm, blissful*) which all have overtones for the reader. The famous last line sums up what Vaughan himself calls inexpressible: that which life touched by the love of God meant to him.

4.4 ANDREW MARVELL

On a Drop of Dew

Summary

ll. 1-8   The poet looks at a pearl-like [or Eastern] dewdrop, shed from the morning on to a blossoming rose. It disregards its new home in favour of the clear region [heaven] from which it comes and which it encloses within itself. So within the limits of its little globe, it reflects as far as it can its native element.

ll. 9-18   The dewdrop seems to slight the purple flower, scarcely touching it in lying there, but gazes back towards the skies, shining sadly as if it wept for itself, because it is for so long separated from the sky. It rolls, restless and insecure, trembling in case it is contaminated [by the earth], until the warm sun pities its suffering and evaporates it back heavenwards.

ll 19-36   So is the human soul a dewdrop, a shining part of the clear fountain of eternity, if it could be seen within the human flower, remembering always the heaven from which it came. It would shun all the leaves and green blossoming of nature, and, gathering to itself [re-collecting; also remembering] its own original light, would, in pure circling thoughts, reveal the greater heaven in the lesser [Heavenlesse is also without heaven]. It winds to and fro in a modest way, turning to shut out the world on every side, but receiving the daylight. So it is dark in its earthly aspect, bright as it looks towards heaven. Disdaining the world, looking in love to heaven, it is loosely attached [to the earth], prepared and ready to ascend, it seems to bend upwards until only a single point touches the world below.

ll. 37-40   So the dew of heaven-sent manna was distilled, white, complete, although cold and congealed. Congealed indeed on earth, but as it is dissolved it [dew, manna and soul] evaporates into the warmth of the all-powerful sun [ascends to God].

Commentary

Marvell's poem is an ingeniously extended Metaphysical conceit, which develops through the poem by a sequence of logical stages. The dewdrop is likened to the Christian soul, which is exactly congruent with it. The poem has two sections, each of eighteen lines, the former describing the dewdrop and the latter the soul; the concluding section of four lines adds the idea of manna, which appeared like dew but like the soul was God-given and returned to God (see Chapter 3). The poem is brilliantly controlled, delicately worked out and beautiful in language, but always subject to the intellect in a style reminiscent of Donne's writing. There is a sense of intellectual enjoyment in the development of the conceit, but it is not an impersonal poem. Marvell, as he often does, distances himself from the emotion he is discussing without deadening it: the poem is not a mere academic exercise, but a lively and intricate analysis of Marvell's vision of the human soul.

Marvell's thesis is that the Christian soul cannot find a fully satisfactory existence on earth any more than can a drop of dew, falling in the morning on the petals of a rose: both must constantly move upwards towards God. Nevertheless, Marvell does not preach an 'other-worldly' religion. As a man, he enjoyed the good things of life in a Cavalier fashion, Puritan in thought though he was, and in his poetry the love of the beauty of nature and the colour of life is very strong. The rose is beautiful, richly coloured (purple is often used interchangeably with red in the seventeenth century) and it blossoms; the world into which the soul comes is full of 'sweet leaves and blossoms green'. It is a beautiful world and a deeply attractive one; Marvell is as aware of this as Herbert was in 'The Pearl', but he shares the older poet's priorities. The aspiration to union with God is paramount.

If the thought is akin to that of Herbert, Marvell's close observation of nature is like that of his contemporary, Henry Vaughan. There are differences: Vaughan looks at the wild nature of the Brecon Beacons, Marvell at the ordered nature of the rose garden, but the sensitivity to beauty and the awareness of the demands of time are the same. The dewdrop's existence is limited by the time before evaporation as the soul's earthly existence is limited by death.

The movement of the poem is dictated in part by the mixture of quatrains and couplets, the latter producing a faster tempo especially when the lines themselves are short; the more reflective lines sustain the four stresses, but have more unstressed syllables and longer vowel sounds (for example, 'For the clear Region where 'twas born' which contrasts with a short, emphatic line such as 'Like its own tear' in which every syllable is stressed). Consonant sounds are also used as support for the meaning and for emphasis: the 'r' sounds in 'Restless it roules' and the 's' sounds in 'Shuns the sweet leaves and blossoms green' add to the sense of movement and of a warm, sighing sound respectively.

Technically, this is one of Marvell's finest poems, intellectually challenging and emotionally satisfying. It combines the stimulating and intricate mental activity of the conceit, reminiscent of Donne, with the delicate observation of nature and lyrical flow of Vaughan. The combination is typical only of Marvell himself.

Bermudas

Summary

ll. 1–4   From a small boat being rowed near the Bermudas, remote and lost in the vast ocean, a song travelled on the listening winds.

ll. 5–28   The song is one of praise to God, Who has led the pilgrims over the pathless waters to an island long undiscovered but much more merciful than their own. There, the huge sea-monsters [whales] which seem to carry the ocean on their backs are stranded.

The pilgrims are safely brought to the grassy banks, safe from both storms and the fury of bishops. God has given them an eternal springtime, with bright enamelled colours; the birds visit them daily, and the oranges shine in the shady trees like golden lamps in a night of green. Pomegranates contain riches more precious than those of Ormus [Hormuz, on the Persian Gulf, associated with great wealth]. Figs seem to come to the pilgrims as food, and melons fall at their feet, and pineapples, so precious that no tree ever has two crops of them.

The land is full of cedars, chosen by God like the cedars of Lebanon, and the sounds of the whales, echoing in the seas, tell of the ambergris on shore [ambergris, a secretion of the sperm whale, was used in making perfume].

ll. 29-36 A much greater cause of boasting by the pilgrims is the pearl of the Gospel, cast with them on the coast. The rocks themselves form a temple in which God's name is to be worshipped. Their voices must be lifted in praise as high as heaven itself, whence they might echo as far as the Bay of Mexico.

ll. 37-40 So the pilgrims in the English boat sang, piously and happily, and in time with their singing, the oars rose and fell.

Commentary

'Bermudas' was presumably written after 1653, when Marvell went to Eton as tutor to Cromwell's ward William Dutton, and stayed at the house of John Oxenbridge, a Fellow of the College. Oxenbridge was a Puritan of firm convictions, who had been persecuted by Archbishop Laud; subsequently, Oxenbridge and his wife (apparently even more Puritanical than her husband) had twice travelled to Bermuda, which was indeed an isle 'so long unknown', having been discovered only in the previous century. No doubt the Oxenbridges told Marvell much about the islands and their beauty (although, perhaps for reasons of tact, no mention is made in the poem of the religious discord which had also arrived there, not least because of Oxenbridge's own intolerance). Literary information was also available, from the mock-epic by Edmund Waller, 'The Battle of the Summer Islands' (another name for the Bermudas), written in 1645. This poem describes a battle between the Bermudas and two whales, and was certainly known to Marvell.

The background of the poem, however, is less interesting than the use Marvell makes of it. The opening and concluding lines suggest that it is a song sung for rowing, echoing the beat of the oars. There is perhaps some truth in this, as the octosyllabic couplets (made up of two rhyming lines with four syllables each) are on the whole regular, and move the poem along in an even way. At the same time, Marvell is too good a poet to have over-emphasised rhythm, and it is subordinate to the poetry rather than to the action described. It is, perhaps, Marvell's most Puritan poem, in that its subject is the Puritan exiles escaping from the rage of Laud (Marvell had little time for him or any other bishop), and that the emphasis is on thanksgiving for safe deliverance and for freedom of worship. In this new island, the Puritans have a ready-made, natural Church and they have brought the Gospel with them; it is 'far kinder' to them than the country they have left behind.

Nevertheless, much the most striking aspect of the poem is not at all Puritanical. Marvell uses his background story to produce a rich, sensuous appreciation of an earthly Paradise, and it is this description which the reader remembers. The sense of colour (especially Marvell's favourite green) is strong, from the richly evocative verb 'enamells' to the orange, gold, green, the overtones of jewels and the fruit he describes. All our senses are involved, from the colour we see to the plentiful fruit we taste and the perfume suggested by ambergris. It is a rich description, made more so by the biblical echoes (cedars of Lebanon), the use of words associated with wealth (*jewels*, *rich*, *price*, *pearl*) and especially the suggestion that the fruit was a gift to the pilgrims: it came to them without their having the labour of picking it. Nature is exotic and bountiful, and Marvell appreciates it with a sense of exhilaration which is much stronger than his fellow-feeling for the Puritans, which was no doubt genuine, but less appealing to his poetic instincts.

To his Coy Mistress

Summary

ll. 1-20   If the world were large enough and time long enough, then the modesty [of the poet's beloved] would not be a crime. They could sit down and debate which way they would walk, and how they would spend their Loves Day [a kind of St Valentine's Day, when lovers were supposed to make up their quarrels] . She could hunt for rubies in India by the river Ganges; he would sit and complain by the river Humber. He would have loved her from before the Flood [the biblical story of Noah's ark; Marvell and his contemporaries would have placed this story historically at about 2300BC] , and she could if she wished go on refusing him until the Jews were converted [to Christianity; this event was popularly supposed to happen just before the end of the world] .

His love would be like a vegetable in growth [it would be characterised only by growth and not by rational sense] , becoming bigger than empires, but even more slowly. [He could spend] a hundred years praising her eyes and gazing on her forehead, two hundred adoring each of her breasts, and thirty thousand years' devotion for the rest of her body. An age [thought of as about eight hundred years] could be devoted to each part of her, and only at the end of time would she show him her heart.

This is the ceremony she deserves, and he would not love her less worthily.

ll. 21-32   But [in the real world] the poet is always conscious of the rapid passing of time, and that before them both there is nothing but the emptiness of eternity. Then, her beauty will no longer exist, nor, in the vaults where her body lies, will his song echo. Only worms will attack the virgin body whose chastity has been preserved for so long, a proud chastity which will itself be dust, as the poet's desire for her will be reduced to ashes. The grave presents a gracious and private setting, but no couple embraces there.

ll. 33-46   Therefore, while she is young and beautiful like the morning, and while her body and spirit respond with desire, they should make love while they can. Now, like birds of prey, they must devour time rather than be slowly chewed to pieces ['chaps' are jaws] by him. All their strength of purpose and their happiness must be summoned up so that the force of their pleasure will tear them through the restraints of life. Thus, while the lovers cannot make the sun [time] stand still, they can triumph in the only way possible [by making him move to their pace].

Commentary

Whether this most justly famous of love lyrics is the result of any personal experience of the poet's, we do not know. Even more than in his 'Definition of Love', Marvell has presented the situation and analysed it with a powerful and compelling emotion while at the same time producing an intellectual scheme (in this case the syllogism, if. . .but. . .therefore) from a distanced standpoint. In its mental agility and complexity of overtones, 'To His Coy Mistress' is like Donne's love poetry, but in its emphasis on time rather than personal relationship, it is different, and more reminiscent of Marvell's own 'Picture of Little T.C'.

Marvell has chosen a common theme, *carpe diem*, take hold of the day, ('gather ye rosebuds') and has coloured it by wide learning from earlier poetry and from the Bible. There is an intellectual pleasure in the awareness of the history of his ideas, quite apart from that to be found in the logical progression of the poem. He echoes Catullus writing to his Lesbia:

> But we, when our brief light has shone,
> Must sleep the long night on and on. (translated by J. Michie)

The Greek writer Aesclepiades wrote of the same theme, telling the reluctant girl:

> You would keep your virginity? What will it profit you? You will find no lover in Hades, girl. (translated by E. M. Parsons)

There are also strong echoes of the Prayer Book burial service:

> . . .we therefore commit his body to the ground; earth to earth,
> ashes to ashes, dust to dust. . .

and of the Bible, with the reference to the sun standing still (Joshua X, 13)
and running (Psalms XIX, 4–6). As with all the Metaphysical poets, Marvell's
knowledge and love of literature, classical and biblical, result in his language
becoming impregnated with references and overtones. It is difficult for a
modern reader to pick up all the associations, but it is important to realise
that they are present, and that the poets' contemporaries would certainly
have recognised them.

But Marvell's poem is far more than the sum of previous knowledge and
ideas. Its outstanding quality is its energy, the tremendous force and surge
of it, the superbly controlled tempo. the range of images, the wit and
humour. Perhaps more than any other poem of the seventeenth century, it
combines the varied qualities of the Metaphysical style, with panache.

The logical pattern, the syllogism referred to, begins with the 'if' ('had
we'), and this first section continues to line 20. The poem starts at what
we might call medium pace, the four stress lines and rhyming couplets
giving movement and, at first, restraint, as the couplets are complete in
themselves. The first premise of the argument is presented. Then the poet's
sense of humour (apart from historical records, the poems themselves
would testify to this quality) takes over, and he builds up his hyperboles
with mounting speed and tension. She should go off to the ends of the
world (India), he would just sit at home (by the Humber) and moan. Love
would be outside the normal limits of time, and his love at least would
grow hugely and slowly; in a delightfully wild conceit, it is a 'vegetable
love'. The poet is now in the territory of the Cavalier compliment (this
poem could never have been written by a Puritan spirit!), adoring the
beauty of each part of his mistress's body, and paying her the delicate but
traditional compliment that she deserves such love, and he will give only
what she deserves.

The second section begins with the kind of recognised shock mentioned in the Commentary on Herbert's 'Redemption', although the content is very different. The poem started with 'if', and so must now have
'but'; we are still unprepared for the enormous effect of the change of
tone. The pace slows (l. 22 has ten syllables, the high number of unstressed
syllables lengthening the line), and Marvell is out of the wild fantasy of the
first section into a reality which is indeed harsh. The famous lines are
wonderfully evocative and spine-chilling. Time, as we say, flies. Whatever
the preoccupations of the moment, behind us time is hurrying and the
inevitable conclusion of time – death – draws nearer. In front of us, eternity
is like a desert, empty and inhospitable, vast and devoid of human comfort.
The word 'all' is beautifully placed, so that its effect irradiates the whole
couplet: the desert is *all* that is before us, it is the *whole* of eternity, it is
before us *all*. By the time the pace begins to accelerate again at line 25, we
are faced with the great metaphysical enemy, time, and aware of its grip

on us. With analytical clarity, Marvell details that desert. Her beauty will go, his love song will be no more. (The sounds and implications of *'marble'*, *'vault'*, *'echoing'* are also as cold as death.) Her body will be deflowered not by the heat of love, but by worms. Her chastity (and the words 'quaint Honour' also meant the female sexual organs) will be dust; his desire for her, ashes. The final couplet of this section is terrifying in its assertion of time (death) as the ending of human love, and also in the combination of the words 'fine' and 'private' (like a bedroom in a stately house) with the word 'grave'. The last twist of the knife in our sensitivies comes with the little sardonic aside, 'I think'.

'Therefore' is the natural conclusion to the two premises, 'if' and 'but'. She is not only beautiful, but she desires him. She is young and has human responses; it is impossible for her (or for us) to forget the chilling inevitability of what has gone before. So let them make love, and so control time, in so far as any human being can do so. The pace slackens for a moment with the renewed threat: time will devour them slowly and nastily. They must gather together all their resources to defeat the power of time with the power of their love. The image may be of a cannonball attacking the gates of a city, or of a sphere (symbol of perfection) breaking out from life and therefore from time. Whatever Marvell's exact picture, we will meet the 'iron gates' later; they are the 'iron wedges' which fate used to prevent the lovers' union in 'The Definition of Love'. Fate, time, death all combine, but the lovers can, albeit temporarily, defeat them all by making all subservient to their desire. The emphasis on 'we will' (four of the first five syllables of the last line are stressed) shows the lovers' determination.

The poem shows the apparent defeat of the enemy, but the enemy's final triumph is assured in the central section, with its cold physical analysis of death producing a physical response in the reader. 'To His Coy Mistress' is, of course, a love poem, on a well-worn theme; its range of emotions and its evocative power make it one of the greatest expressions in English poetry of the opposition basic in human life: love versus death.

The Definition of Love

Summary

1. The origins of the poet's love are as strange as its object is remote from him: its parents are despair and impossibility.

2. Only high-minded despair could produce such a divine offering, while a feeble-minded hope could do nothing more than flap its gaudy wings without flight.

3. It might have been possible for the poet to achieve what his soul is directed towards, had fate not driven an iron wedge between [the lovers] forcing its way in to divide them.

4. For fate looks jealously at two perfect loves and will not let them

unite. Their union would spell its ruin and destroy its tyrannical power.

5. Therefore fate's decree, as strong as steel, has placed the lovers as far apart as the poles, and although the whole world of love turns on them, they cannot embrace each other.

6. Unless the heavens become dizzy and collapse, and the world is torn by some new earthquake or, in order to unite the lovers, is flattened into a planisphere [a flat, two-dimensional projection of the world].

7. Duller love, like oblique lines, may be united at every corner, but loves which, like straight lines, are truly parallel, may last for ever without union.

8. So the love which so truly unites the lovers but which is prevented from fulfilment by fate, is a coming together of the minds and a separation by the stars.

Commentary

Of all Marvell's poems, this is the one which most clearly reminds the reader of Donne; the resemblance to the 'Valediction: forbidding mourning' is strong both in poetic form (rhythm and rhyme) and in theme (the absence of the beloved). Yet 'The Definition of Love' is Marvell's and not Donne's, and even a first glance shows some of the differences. Donne's poem is about a personal love, and he uses immediate, simple language ('so let us melt'; 'such wilt thou be to mee') as well as a logical framework and, of course, the famous imagery.

Marvell, as his title tells us, is *defining* love. He presents the situation: he knows the impoossibility of the fulfilment of his love, and he feels despair. The poem has a strongly logical, intellectual pattern, but there is no development. The rightness of despair is shown, the inevitable futility of hope, the quality within the love itself which in an imperfect world makes a perfect love impossible and, in conclusion, the union which exists only because the lovers are apart (which was the cause of his despair at the beginning). Marvell stands back from the emotion of love to discuss the qualities and the destiny of this particular kind of love. His manner is formal and lacks the dramatic intensity of Donne's involvement.

Yet Marvell's poem is not without emotion. Strangely, it is the very restraint and distancing which give the poem its power, what T. S. Eliot called Marvell's 'tough reasonableness beneath the slight lyric grace'. We become aware of the logical inevitability of the poem through the poet's definition of the situation, and so we feel a compassion not so much for the immediate suffering (if there was any) but for the imperfection of human love and the impossibility of a perfect human love, and we have no doubt about the necessity of such a compassion.

Nevertheless, in technique as in form, Marvell is influenced by Donne's poem. The logical development of images is similar: fate's envy, strong actions (driving the iron wedges), awareness that love has in it the possibility of overturning fate itself. Fate becomes almost a character in the poem, the enemy of love as absence is potentially the enemy of love in Donne's 'Valediction'. The image of the parallel lines, although not developed as fully as that of the compasses, is of the same type, a mathematical proof of an aspect of love. Marvell's poem is full of antitheses: the 'yet...but', 'for...and therefore', 'as...but...'pattern shows the logical contrasts by which the poetry proceeds. There is deliberate play on words: 'extended' means 'held out to' and also 'stretched to its limit'; 'fixt' is the goal to which the soul is directed and also its firmness. In the last verse, the astrological image is duplicated in the lovers: the conjunction of the stars is an apparent union (within the same sign of the zodiac), and such is the union of the two lovers' minds; the opposition of the stars (representing fate) is the two heavenly bodies at opposite points (180° apart), and such is the lack of physical union of the lovers.

Perhaps the most striking use of words in the poem is the 'magnanimous Despair', a bringing together of apparently contradictory expressions which is known as an *oxymoron*. Marvell contrasts two examples of this technique – the one quoted, with 'feeble hope', (hope being usually thought of as indicative of strength of character) and this juxtaposition is the main thesis of the poem. In an imperfect world, ideal love is impossible, and therefore a high-minded, resolute despair is more appropriate than a weak and pointless hope. The final irony is that the love was begotten by such despair; had despair and impossibility not both been present, there would have been no such love.

The Picture of little T. C. in a Prospect of Flowers

Summary
1. See how simply this nymph [the child] begins her golden life! She loves to lie on the green grass, and there by her beauty tames the wild flowers, giving them names. She plays only with the roses, telling them which colour and what smell suits them best.

2. Who can foresee for what great purposes such a darling of the gods was born? Yet this same child will grow into one whose chastity will be feared by the wanton god of love [Cupid], for under her severe command, his bow will be broken and his flags of war torn.

3. The poet must, then, come to terms and negotiate with her conquering eyes in good time, before they have tried out their power to wound, or been driven in careless triumph over yearning hearts, despising all the more those which surrender. He will be laid where he can watch her glories from a safe distance.

4. Meanwhile, as all green nature is charmed by her beauty, she must continue to put right the errors of the springtime; she can make sure that the tulips have a rightful share of sweetness as well as beauty,

disarm the roses of their thorns, but most of all bring it about that the violets last longer.

5. She is a young beauty of the woods to whom nature pays tribute with fruit and flowers. The flowers she may gather, but the buds should be spared, lest Flora [goddess of flowers], angry at the crime of killing her young ones in their prime, make an example of *her* and, before anyone notices, nip in the bud all her family's [and the poet's] hopes, and the child herself.

Commentary

On the surface, 'Little T.C.' is a poem of Elizabethan simplicity and grace, a pastoral scene of spring flowers with a little girl playing happily, a girl who will one day become a beauty of devastating power and coquetry. It is indeed a pleasing prospect, as 'prospect' suggests an attractive landscape. But the word 'prospect' has overtones of the future, a kind of mental looking forward to future destiny, and as so often in Marvell's poetry, the future enemy is death. Beneath its pleasing surface, 'Little T.C.' is a poem about time, with a considerable sense of apprehension, almost fear. Marvell's great achievement is to bind the two levels together so skilfully that we accept and respond to both. It has rightly been called a poem of innocence which becomes a poem of experience.

This movement begins with the lightest of touches in the first verse. The girl is a nymph, the day is golden as is her future, the grass green (a favourite colour of the poet's, with all its overtones of freshness, spring-time, new life and energy), the roses are in bloom. Nevertheless, the child is already growing in sophistication; she 'names' the flowers (she is in control of them) and she dictates their colour and smell. Her power is already asserted, even if mainly in her own imagination.

The girl's sophistication will develop, and she will one day wage war against Cupid himself, with her militant virtue triumphant. So far, her progress is that of any attractive, well-born girl, but in the third verse there is a transition from pastoral ease and charm. The poet issues a warning, and introduces the darker side of his enemy, time. Military imagery, used lightly in the previous verse, now becomes stronger; he will have to come to terms with her conquering eyes now, before they can inflict real wounds. The sense of impending pain is too immediate for the lyricism which has gone before: the wounds are real, and those who suffer may be trampled on (driven over) and despised for their suffering. The child may have not just a militant virtue, but also the ability to inflict a deeply-felt pain – and she may use that ability. The danger inherent in the beauty which merely commands flowers to obey (at present) is clear.

Time has moved on for the poet, too. When she is sufficiently grown up to cause pain, he may be able only to watch from the side-lines. The suggestion of death is too clear in the 'time', 'let me be laid', 'shade' sequence to be accidental. Time will bring not only sophistication but his death. The poem has moved from innocence into experience, and the return to the child and the flowers in the fourth verse is now coloured by the knowledge of death. So we are prepared for the awareness of the brief life of the violets, and it is with a sense of doom that we read the last verse where the picking of the floral buds merges with the death of the child. The possibility that time may be defeated by death has grown into the poet's and the reader's awareness. If, as is suggested, 'T. C.' was Theophila Cornewall, daughter of friends of the poet, there is an additional irony: she was the second child to bear the name, the first born, as often happened, dying shortly after birth. The very name 'Theophila', meaning 'loved by the gods', is ironic.

There is a fresh lyrical grace to the poem with its long verses bound by rhyme and given additional emphasis by the short line/long line technique at the end of the verse: the long five-stressed final line carries in each case the developing thought, leading into the next verse until the explicit fear of death at the close of the poem.

Marvell wrote more complex and more famous poems than 'Little T.C.', but it is in its own way perfect, blending the grace of the courtly love poem with the intellect and the realism of the best of Metaphysical poetry.

An Horatian Ode upon Cromwell's Return from Ireland

Summary

ll. 1-8   The youth who would be ready for the demands of the time must now put aside his poetic inspiration [the Muses were nine goddesses who inspired the arts], and not stay in the shadows singing his love poetry. It is time to leave books to gather dust, and instead oil the armour, rusty with lack of use, removing it from its decorative place on the walls.

ll. 9-24   So the restless Cromwell could not be at ease in the peaceful arts which bring no glory, but pursued his destiny through warlike ventures. As the three-forked lightning first breaks through the clouds whence it comes, so he forced his way through his own party, for rivals and enemies are all alike to high courage, and it is harder to contain such a one than to oppose him. He then burnt his way through the elements, destroying palaces and temples on his way, until at last he struck Caesar's head in spite of its laurel wreath [laurel was popularly supposed to be proof against lightning].

ll. 25-44   It would be madness either to resist or to blame the flash of heaven's lightning, and, to speak truly, much is due to Cromwell himself. From his private gardens, where he had lived a reserved, austere life as if his greatest achievement was to plant pear trees [the bergamot is a type of pear known as 'the pear of kings'], he climbed by dedication and courage to the position from which he could destroy what had been built up over centuries, and refashion the ancient kingdom. Justice might complain against fate, pleading the rights given over the ages, but in vain: these hold true or break as the men who wield them are strong or weak. Nature hates a vacuum, but even more cannot allow two bodies to be in the same place at the same time, and therefore [the lesser] must make room when the greater spirit comes on the scene.

ll. 45-56　There is no battle in the Civil War in which Cromwell's scars are not the deepest. The affair of Hampton Court shows too how cunning he could be, when, mingling fear and hope, he wove a net so subtly that Charles was persuaded to hurry himself to the close prison of Carisbrooke. From there, the royal actor was taken, to mount his tragic scaffold [the 'scaffold' was both a place of execution and the stage] while around him armed soldiers clapped their bloodstained hands.

ll. 57-72　[Charles] did nothing which was low or degrading on that memorable occasion, but tested the edge of the axe with his keen eyesight. He did not with cheap bitterness call on the gods to vindicate the righteousness of his cause, but bowed his handsome head low as if in bed. This was the memorable moment which confirmed the power which had been achieved by force. It was like that in which [as the Roman historian Livy records] the building of the temple to Juniper on the Capitol [in Rome] was begun; the excavators found a human head which scared away the builders, but which was seen as a good omen for the State.

ll. 73-90　Now the Irish are ashamed to see themselves subdued in one year [Cromwell's 1649-50 campaign, in which he savagely 'tamed' the Irish]. So much can one man do who is capable of both action and understanding. They [i.e., those he has defeated] can best praise him and in defeat testify how good and just he is, and fit for the highest office. Nor has he grown autocratic in command, but keeps himself always at the republic's disposal; one who can so well obey others is fit also to rule. As his first year's rent, he presents a kingdom to the Commons, and holds back his own reputation so that it may become theirs. His sword and the spoils of war have been put aside and laid at the feet of the people.

ll. 91-112　So the falcon which has flown high falls steeply from the skies; having killed, she ceases to search [for prey], but perches on the nearest green bough. When he has lured her so far, the falconer is sure of trapping her.

What then may England not hope for, while Cromwell's helmet is crested with such victory? Others may indeed be afraid, if he crowns every year in this way. He has come as Caesar to Gaul, as Hannibal to Italy [i.e., as a conqueror], and will bring a new epoch to all states which are not free. The Picts [Scots] shall find no shelter in their treacherous minds [a pun on parti-coloured and party-coloured] , but will shrink under their plaids at such solemn valour. They will be happy if the tufted bracken camouflages them from the English hunter, so that his dogs are not put on the scent of the Caledonian [Scottish] deer.

ll.113–120 But Cromwell, child of war and fortune, must go forward without wearying, and to the end must keep his sword drawn. Apart from the authority it has to frighten the spirits of the dead [of the Civil War, including Charles himself] , it must help him to maintain the power which was won by the sword.

Commentary

This is the most famous and probably the greatest poem of the Civil War. It was written in the summer of 1650, scarcely eighteen months after the execution of King Charles I, which Marvell had opposed. Cromwell, who was not yet personally known to the poet, had just returned from his Irish campaign (in spite of Marvell's tribute, the campaign was a bloody and vicious one), and was about to set off for Scotland (which was threatening to recognise Charles II as king). This was the expedition which General Fairfax, subsequently Marvell's benefactor, refused to lead.

Officially, the poem appears as a eulogy of Cromwell, a formal, stately ode to Cromwell's glory. In fact, it is a study of the ambiguities of power, considered, balanced and intelligent. Marvell has succeeded in combining a traditional 'triumphant' poem with a courageous and objective evaluation not only of Cromwell himself, but of all who wield power in the state. He takes as his models the classical poets Horace and Lucan, sharing the former's sense of the ambiguity of power. The metre, which Marvell used only for this poem, is an essentially iambic octosyllabic couplet (two rhyming lines with four stresses each), with short interludes of hexasyllabic (six syllable) couplets. It is extremely successful in suggesting both a rapid movement of events and a stately inevitability, the complexity of the issues and a grave appraisal of public affairs. These very qualities contributed to the censorship which the poem suffered. It was cancelled from the 1681 edition of Marvell's poems, presumably for political reasons, and was not published again until 1776.

The poem begins with a warlike call to a military life as opposed to one of music and poetry; it is a strong opening influenced by Marvell's Roman models, but very soon Cromwell is introduced in terms which produce mixed feelings. Lines 9 and 10 suggest that war is glorious, peaceful skills are not, and that Cromwell was restless while he pursued peace. Even allowing for the martial beginning of the poem, it is obvious that the writer, an expert in the arts of peace, must call them 'inglorious' with a certain amount of irony. The double-edged meanings become more pronounced. Cromwell, like lightning, broke through his own party, showing his high courage. Marvell suggests that his hero is an elemental force, beyond the limits of human control, acting like an agent of the gods. At the same time, lightning is destructive and without mercy; those who will use violence indiscriminately on their own side as well as against an enemy are not usually attractive figures. It is difficult to accept, and Marvell intends us to find it so, that courage can be as careless of the consequences to its own rivals as it is to those of its opponents.

Nevertheless, Marvell builds up a picture of the inevitability of Cromwell's destiny. The classical references help to suggest historical necessity: Caesar, in spite of his laurel wreaths of victory, had to fall (but compare 1. 101, when Cromwell himself is given the title 'Caesar'). Cromwell is 'Heavens flame' and so destined to overcome everything in his way. The poet then moves to a consideration of Cromwell as a human being. He sees him as a man content to live quietly and austerely in the country (Cromwell had been a farmer), until called to employ his courage and his resources to bring about a change in the form of government of his country. The ambiguity is clearly shown in the poet's use of the word 'ruine': if Charles (or the institution of the monarchy, or both) was 'the great work of time', then the ruin of that work is to be deprecated. The note of censure continues as Marvell sees the struggle as one of justice against fate: Cromwell has already been firmly established as fate, which leaves the justice to Charles. It is true that Marvell makes the maintenance of the 'ancient rights' depend on the strength of the man who holds them, but they are nevertheless depicted as 'rights', historically held. Charles had been unable to maintain his rights: Cromwell had taken them over, as the stronger man inevitably must, but the picture is certainly not one-sided. The section ends with a typically Metaphysical scientific image.

Cromwell's public qualities are next discussed. He has been a good soldier, and Marvell's admiration for his personal courage is unqualified. It was amply shown in the Civil War. However, Cromwell combines a devious political ability with his military prowess. The story current at the time was that Cromwell had deliberately frightened Charles into going to Carisbrooke Castle on the Isle of Wight in the belief that he had friends there: the fact of his flight was then used as propaganda against him. History has thrown doubt on this episode, but Marvell probably did not question it, showing his own attitude to such deceit by the use of words like 'net', 'case' (plight as well as prison) and 'art' (with its overtones of cunning).

The focus of the poem shifts to Charles. There is a note of self-dramatisation in the description of the King in theatrical terms, but the famous lines draw a picture which is extremely sympathetic. He is seen as the hero of a tragedy and therefore noble, courageous, greater in nature than ordinary men. The soldiers around clapped their bloodstained hands (with joy at his downfall or in admiration of his nobility? We do not know). Charles himself behaved with great dignity, not asserting himself loudly or lessening the appeal of his majesty; he bowed his head (the emphasis is on the word 'down' with its gentle, featherbed overtones) to the axe. So power – Cromwell's power – is asserted, but by force, and the good omen for the future of the State is based on the death of Charles (the 'bleeding head') rather than on the virtues of the new regime.

The poem moves back to Cromwell, his victories, his justice, his willingness always to act in the State's interest rather than his own. The words are full of praise, but they lack the vividness with which Charles' end was described, and are therefore coloured by what has gone before. At l. 91, Marvell begins to look to the future with a clear-sighted and sombre gaze. As the falcon is most vulnerable when it has just killed, so Cromwell is now most likely to be attacked, and the image carries both a spur (Cromwell must continue his warlike progress) and a warning (bloodshed leads inevitably to further bloodshed). The leader's destiny is to bring glory to his country, but only through fear and the use of force. He is now Caesar, and by implication as likely to fall as Charles was at l. 23. The Scots, who had negotiated with Charles while he was at Carisbrooke, were Cromwell's next victims. Marvell shows little concern for them, and indeed is scathing at what he perceives as their treacherous nature. (There is a complex pun on the word 'Pict' and its possible derivation from the Latin verb *pingere*, to paint; this suggests both a primitive and savage people who used warpaint and cowards who wanted camouflage. The spelling 'party-coloured' also suggests a people who were likely to change sides to suit themselves.)

The ending of the poem is as solemn and formal as a triumphal ode requires, but it retains the critical judgement of the earlier lines. Cromwell is heir to war and fortune; he has a harsh as well as a glorious destiny. His sword must always be drawn, indeed held erect and so cross-hilted as if to frighten away evil spirits. Its power has to be used against both the living and the dead. A power won at the cost of civil war will have to be maintained at the cost of further bloodshed.

Given its date, the poem is remarkably objective and balanced. Marvell admires Cromwell, admires too the cause which he leads ('too good to have been fought for', he describes it, tellingly), and feels that destiny has chosen Cromwell almost against his will for such an office. At the same time, the poet pays tribute to Charles, not for his cause but for his courage, respecting the dignity of the King as he faced death. Most interestingly, Marvell looks at power and its demands on those who achieve it and those who retain it. Cromwell is viewed critically and in many ways the final impression is of a harsh valour; he is also warned, with clear judgement and strong personal feeling, of the fate of those who live by the sword. In the combination of intellectual analysis and word-play, the poem belongs to the Metaphysical tradition; in its ambivalent attitude to contemporary political events, it is Marvell's own.

5 CRITICAL RECEPTION

It is probably true to say that all four Metaphysical poets, after initial popularity and esteem, sank into near-obscurity, were remembered, if at all, for qualities which now seem surprising, and came back to full recognition towards the end of the nineteenth and in the early twentieth centuries. Since then, they have been regarded as among the greatest of English poets.

During his lifetime, Donne's poems were circulated in manuscript to a London-based circle of educated men; generally, he was much more widely known as a preacher. The poet Thomas Carew (1594–1640) claimed to write the first elegy to Donne after his death in 1631; it contained an accurate picture of the writing of the 'Deane of Pauls' as original in thought and in use of language, combining 'deepe knowledge' with 'rich and pregnant phansie' (imagination). Donne's position as leader of the 'Metaphysical school' was established in Carew's reference to his rule of 'the universall Monàrchy of wit'. Within forty years of Donne's death, seven printed editions of his poetry had appeared, testifying to its popularity and impact.

George Herbert's poetry, likewise originally circulated in manuscript, was published to general acclaim within a year of his death. Henry Vaughan testified in his published work to the influence of Herbert, and his own writing was received with interest in the 1650s.

Andrew Marvell's poems were first published posthumously in 1681, with the exception, presumably for political reasons, of the 'Horatian Ode'.

By the time of Andrew Marvell's death, public taste was already turning away from Metaphysical poetry. Abraham Cowley (1618–67), considered in the eighteenth century to be the greatest of Metaphysical poets, commented in 'Of Wit' that in poetry too much wit is undesirable, and reason should always be in control. Cowley was a scientist as well as a poet, and poetry moved away from the imagery and drama of earlier years towards ordered social comment and satire. It was the poet John Dryden, writing in 1693, who disparagingly used the word 'metaphysics' in connection with Donne, accusing him of speculating on philosophy rather than entertaining 'the fair sex' in his love poetry. Regularity of verse form and balanced comment was favoured; typically, the great poet of the new age, Alexander Pope (1688-1744) 'versified', that is, made regular, some of Donne's satires to achieve a greater smoothness of flow.

Samuel Johnson (1709-84), essayist and critic, in his *Life of Cowley*, 1779, condemned the Metaphysical poets as men of learning whose 'whole endeavour' was to show that learning. He claimed that they wrote 'rather as beholders than partakers of human nature', a judgement which seems incredible to twentieth-century eyes, but which was influential, although not undisputed, until the late nineteenth century.

For almost two centuries, Metaphysical poetry was either forgotten (especially, in the eighteenth century, the work of Henry Vaughan) or anthologised, a few 'respectable' poems appearing on public view. George Herbert retained some popularity as a pious writer (although his verses were also 'regularised' and their impact muted), and Andrew Marvell, first seen primarily as a politician and then as a nature poet, was known for a small number of poems; the adjectives most often used of his work were graceful, delicate, charming, natural, unaffected: unusual words for so discriminating and urbane a poet.

Nevertheless, some nineteenth-century poets and critics appreciated and admired a wider range of Metaphysical poetry. Samuel Taylor Coleridge wrote of 'the sense of novelty and freshness with old and familiar objects', and summed up delightfully the controlled courtesy of Herbert's poetry: 'The scholar and the poet supplies the material, but the perfect well-bred gentleman the expression and arrangement.' Donne was admired by Robert Browning, Vaughan respected as a precursor of William Wordsworth, Marvell was sensitively appreciated by Gerard Manley Hopkins. However, it was the critic Herbert Grierson, editing Donne's poems in 1912 and a wider range of Metaphysical poetry in 1921, who first analysed the poetry in what we would call 'modern' terms. Grierson identified two dominant strains in Donne's love poetry: 'the subtle play of argument and wit, erudite and fantastic', and 'the strain of vivid realism. . .love as an actual, immediate experience in all its moods'. The same perceptive critic commented on Vaughan's 'occasional sublimity of imaginative vision' and, later, analysed Marvell's poetry as 'passionate, paradoxical argument, touched with humour and learned imagery'.

If Grierson founded the modern view of Metaphysical poetry, it was T. S. Eliot who drew widespread attention in the 1920s to the work of Donne and Marvell. To his essays belong many of the best-known comments: 'A thought to Donne was an experience; it modified his sensibility', and, of Metaphysical wit; 'It involves, probably, a recognition, implicit in the expression of every experience, of other kinds of experience which are possible'. Eliot's essays are less influential now, perhaps because they are less needed. The contemporary critic J. B. Leishman has referred to Donne's tenderness and wit, Vaughan's 'white ecstasy', Herbert's passionate personal drama, and to Marvell's poetry as 'the poetry of a temperament. . . in which nearly all the most attractive virtues of the earlier seventeenth century seem to be combined'. Perhaps the unity of experience and the sheer energy referred to in the first chapter of this book attract the late-twentieth-century reader; there is certainly no sign that the attraction is in decline.

REVISION QUESTIONS

1. 'Metaphysical imagery...is used as a means of communicating thoughts and of exploring experience and achieving new insight into it' (J. Dalglish). Examine the poetry of John Donne in the light of this statement.

2. Analyse any one secular *and* one religious poem by John Donne, showing similarities and differences in imagery, diction and rhythm.

3. Examine 'exquisite tact' as a quality in the poetry of George Herbert.

4. 'The one explores, the other reveals' (D. J. Enright). Examine this analysis of the difference between the poetry of John Donne and that of George Herbert.

5. Both mystic and social commentator. Discuss these aspects of the poetry of Henry Vaughan.

6. Compare the treatment of nature in the poems of Henry Vaughan and Andrew Marvell.

7. T. S. Eliot described the poetry of Andrew Marvell as having 'tough reasonableness beneath the slight lyric grace'. Discuss the accuracy of this description.

8. Discuss the relationship between God and man as revealed in any two of the four poets.

9. 'To speak familiarly of ultimate things is the prerogative of the Metaphysical Poets' (Joan Bennett). Discuss, with particular reference to the work of any one of the four poets.

10. 'The intellect was at the tip of the senses' (T. S. Eliot). Show how this is true of either John Donne or Andrew Marvell.

11. Examine the treatment of love by any one of the four poets.

12. The outstanding characteristic of the Metaphysical poets is energy. Discuss 'energy' in the poetry of any two of the four poets.

FURTHER READING

Texts

Dalgish, Jack (ed.), *Eight Metaphysical Poets* (Heinemann, 1961). The above edition forms the basis of this book. It keeps the old forms of spelling sufficiently to give the flavour of seventeenth-century poetry, without creating unnecessary difficulties for the modern reader. The introduction is helpful, and there are useful short biographies of the poets.

Hayward, John (ed.), *Donne: Complete Poetry and Selected Prose* (The Nonesuch Press, 1978). A comprehensive view of Donne's poetry, and a useful introduction to the *Sermons* and *Letters*.

Smith, A. J. (ed.), *John Donne: The Complete English Poems* (Penguin, 1971).

Rudrum, Alan (ed.), *Henry Vaughan: The Complete Poems* (Penguin, 1976).

Donno, E. S. (ed.), *Andrew Mar]ell: The Complete Poems* (Penguin, 1972).

The above three Penguin editions are available for all who want to read more than the standard poems. The notes in each case are very helpful.

Criticism

Beer, Patricia, *An Introduction to the Metaphysical Poets* (Macmillan, 1972).

Bennett, Joan, *Five Metaphysical Poets* (Cambridge University Press, 1964). Contains chapters on Donne, Herbert, Vaughan, Crashaw and Marvell.

Eliot, T. S. 'The Metaphysical Poets' and 'Andrew Marvell' in *Selected Essays* (Faber, 1932).

Leishman, J. B., *The Monarch of Wit*, 5th edition (Hutchinson, 1962).

The Pelican Guide to English Literature, 3: From Donne to Marvell (Pelican, 1982), with later revisions. An excellent collection of essays on individual poets, with helpful background and links with European literature.

Walton, Izaak, *Lives* (World's Classics, 1927). First published between 1640 and 1670, Walton's *Lives* of Donne and Herbert were the earliest biographies, and personal in tone: Walton was friend and parishioner of Donne. They are sometimes prejudiced by what the author wanted to believe, but they give vivid, contemporary and very readable insights into the two poets. Sadly, the book is out of print and difficult to obtain, but available in scholarly libraries.

Mastering English Literature
Richard Gill

Mastering English Literature will help readers both to enjoy English Literature and to be successful in 'O' levels, 'A' levels and other public exams. It is an introduction to the study of poetry, novels and drama which helps the reader in four ways - by providing ways of approaching literature, by giving examples and practice exercises, by offering hints on how to write about literature, and by the author's own evident enthusiasm for the subject. With extracts from more than 200 texts, this is an enjoyable account of how to get the maximum satisfaction out of reading, whether it be for formal examinations or simply for pleasure.

Work Out English Literature ('A' level)
S.H. Burton

This book familiarises 'A' level English Literature candidates with every kind of test which they are likely to encounter. Suggested answers are worked out step by step and accompanied by full author's commentary. The book helps students to clarify their aims and establish techniques and standards so that they can make appropriate responses to similar questions when the examination pressures are on. It opens up fresh ways of looking at the full range of set texts, authors and critical judgements and motivates students to know more of these matters.

THE MACMILLAN SHAKESPEARE

General Editor: PETER HOLLINDALE
Advisory Editor: PHILIP BROCKBANK

The Macmillan Shakespeare features:
* clear and uncluttered texts with modernised punctuation and spelling wherever possible;
* full explanatory notes printed on the page facing the relevant text for ease of reference;
* stimulating introductions which concentrate on content, dramatic effect, character and imagery, rather than mere dates and sources.

Above all, The Macmillan Shakespeare treats each play as a work for the theatre which can also be enjoyed on the page.

CORIOLANUS
Editor: Tony Parr

THE WINTER'S TALE
Editor: Christopher Parry

MUCH ADO ABOUT NOTHING
Editor: Jan McKeith

RICHARD II
Editor: Richard Adams

RICHARD III
Editor: Richard Adams

HENRY IV, PART I
Editor: Peter Hollindale

HENRY IV, PART II
Editor: Tony Parr

HENRY V
Editor: Brian Phythian

AS YOU LIKE IT
Editor: Peter Hollindale

A MIDSUMMER NIGHT'S DREAM
Editor: Norman Sanders

THE MERCHANT OF VENICE
Editor: Christopher Parry

THE TAMING OF THE SHREW
Editor: Robin Hood

TWELFTH NIGHT
Editor: E. A. J. Honigmann

THE TEMPEST
Editor: A. C. Spearing

ROMEO AND JULIET
Editor: James Gibson

JULIUS CAESAR
Editor: D. R. Elloway

MACBETH
Editor: D. R. Elloway

HAMLET
Editor: Nigel Alexander

ANTONY AND CLEOPATRA
Editors: Jan McKeith and
Richard Adams

OTHELLO
Editors: Celia Hilton and R. T. Jones

KING LEAR
Editor: Philip Edwards